Praise for Graeme Simsion

'Ranks with the best romantic comedies of our age.'
Globe and Mail on *The Rosie Project*

'Quietly profound.'
Independent on *The Rosie Project*

'[Don Tillman is] one of the most endearing, charming and
fascinating literary characters I have met in a long time.'
The Times on *The Rosie Effect*

'As smart, funny and heartwarming as the original.'
Washington Post on *The Rosie Effect*

'Fiction as good as it gets…Laugh-out-loud funny.'
New York Times on *The Rosie Result*

'Behind all the steady wit, the rolling jokes…
this is a thoughtful and provocative novel.'
Age on *The Rosie Result*

'A great read—romantic, wry and well-written.'
Daily Mail on *The Best of Adam Sharp*

'A hugely romantic tale…Some of it is quite lovely and
moving; some of it is funny and much of it is unsettling.'
Daily Review on *The Best of Adam Sharp*

'A beautifully crafted tale of love, self-acceptance and blisters.'
Sunday Express on *Two Steps Forward* (with Anne Buist)

'An escapist, gently witty read.'
West Australian on *Two Steps Onward* (with Anne Buist)

'The only genuinely readable book in my library
on the often dry subject of data modelling.'
Applied Information Science on *Data Modeling Essentials*

The Novel Project

The Novel Project

A step-by-step guide to your novel, memoir or biography

Graeme Simsion

TEXT PUBLISHING MELBOURNE AUSTRALIA

The Text Publishing Company acknowledges the Traditional Owners of the country on which we work, the Wurundjeri people of the Kulin Nation, and pays respect to their Elders past and present.

textpublishing.com.au

The Text Publishing Company
Wurundjeri Country, Level 6, Royal Bank Chambers, 287 Collins Street, Melbourne Victoria 3000 Australia

The Text Publishing Company (UK) Ltd
130 Wood Street, London EC2V 6DL, United Kingdom

Published by The Text Publishing Company, 2022

Cover design by Chong W.H.
Page design by Imogen Stubbs
Illustrations on pages 13, 15 and 58 by Simon Barnard
Typeset by J&M Typesetting

Printed and bound in Australia by Griffin Press, part of Ovato, an accredited ISO/NZS 14001:2004 Environmental Management System printer.

ISBN: 9781922458384 (paperback)
ISBN: 9781922459695 (ebook)

A catalogue record for this book is available from the National Library of Australia.

To my teachers

CONTENTS

PART I: PREPARATION

1. Overview	3
The problem with pantsing	4
A novel as a project	5
Basic principles	8
How this book is organised	10
How long will it take?	12
Tailoring the process	16
What about being an artist?	18
2. Being a Writer	21
Becoming a professional writer	22
Writing life and habits	24
Dealing with rejection	31
Dealing with success	34
3. Creativity	35
Harnessing your creativity	36
Principles and techniques	38
Routine physical activities	38
Focus	39
Experiment with combinations	40
Breaking the rules	40
Incubation period	40
Solutions create new problems—and opportunities	42
You can always make it better	43
Two heads	44
Other creativity techniques	45
On getting stuck	46

4. Structure   49

How to use structure   51

The language of structure   52

The three-act structure   56

Beyond the three-act structure   62

PART II: PROCESS

5. Concept   67

Writing what you know   71

The quest for originality   75

Biography and memoir   79

Reviewing your concept   81

     Is the concept big enough?   81

     Can you do the research?   82

     Appropriation—can you tell this story?   82

     What's special about your concept?   83

Case study   84

6. Synopsis—Plot   87

Trying it out   89

Tips on writing a draft synopsis   89

7. Synopsis—Characters and Character   95

Drawing on real life   96

Focusing on decisions   98

Character arcs   106

Making characters relatable   107

More characters   111

Names   113

Combining characters   114

Case study   115

8. Brainstorming the Story — 117

Research — 119

Structure and point of view — 121

Types of cards: scene, summary, pause and ellipsis — 123

Coming up with cards — 125

Organising the cards—first cut — 134

9. Organising the Story — 137

Structure — 137

Laying out your story — 138

Reviewing the acts — 140

Reviewing the first act — 141

Reviewing the second act — 142

Reviewing the third act — 146

Reviewing the full story — 147

10. Reviewing the Outline — 151

11. First Draft—Process — 157

How many words per day? — 159

Overview of the process — 160

Planning your writing day — 163

12. First Draft—Content — 169

13. Rewriting — 181

Reviewing the big picture — 182

Where to focus — 183

What to look for — 186

Beta readers — 190

Wrapping up — 193

14. Working with Your Editor — 195

Acknowledgments — 201

PART I
Preparation

1
Overview

'**Writing is easy:** all you do is sit staring at a blank sheet of paper until drops of blood form on your forehead.' Variously attributed to Thomas Wolfe, Paul Gallico and Ernest Hemingway, the quote portrays writing as mysterious, torturous and, implicitly, unteachable.

This book is about another approach, based on established theories of creativity and design, and on the experience of authors, including me, who—preferring to save the drama for the story—have adopted a more structured and reliable process.

It's aimed at those who want to write a book for publication, or at least one that others will want to read. If you're writing primarily for yourself—for self-discovery, therapy or the pure pleasure of working with language—then some of my advice may not be relevant to you. That said, if you're aiming to produce a finished manuscript at some point, read on.

But first, let's take a brief look at the 'drops of blood' version. Many writers are committed—often unbendingly so—to making the story up as they go, unaware of how it will unfold and what the ending will be. Writing by the seat of their pants. *Pantsing*, they call it.

The problem with pantsing

Some very successful novelists identify as pantsers. Why wouldn't they? Creating a compelling story that will make the reader laugh, cry or gasp in surprise at the unexpected twist; setting up and resolving subplots; inventing believable characters and sub-textual themes; describing the world in a way that makes us see it anew; and doing it all in elegant, memorable prose, on the fly, is a pretty impressive trick—a sign of a special talent, if not genius. Trouble is, most of us are not geniuses.

If you go down the pantser route without the capability, there's every chance you won't write a publishable novel (or memoir or biography—more about this later in the chapter). You'll spend a lot of time staring at the page—perhaps the first page, perhaps the fiftieth—waiting for the words to come.

Some authors manage to get about a third of a book down before the inspiration dries up. They may do it again and again, practising what they can do (setting up a story, writing fine prose) without coming to grips with what they can't (keeping a story moving to a satisfying ending).

Sometimes they struggle on, and, as readers, we've seen the results: novels that engage us at first, then lose their way. I've met a few authors who've pulled off the pantser approach once, then struck the difficult-second-novel problem. I suspect that the first novel had spent years in the writer's head, where their subconscious had laid down an outline. Or perhaps it was based on real events, as many debuts are, so the storyline and characters were already established.

If your attention is on each sentence as it comes rather than the (unknown) big picture, you can expect the result to be stronger on prose than on story. If that prose is good enough, perhaps the book will make it in the world of literary fiction, where story is seen by some to be less important. But unless it wins a major prize, don't expect the royalties to pay the bills. And using fine words to tell an uninteresting, unimportant or unengaging story seems like an opportunity lost.

Writing courses almost always focus on prose. Students workshop, and are assessed on, pieces of a few thousand words. But many struggle to scale up their sometimes beautiful and powerful writing into a novel.

Why is it so hard? One of the reasons we underestimate the difficulty is that almost everybody can tell stories. Every day we relate events to our colleagues and friends; we may hold their rapt attention as we tell them about the time we stayed after the Bruce Springsteen concert to watch the band pack up…for a few *minutes*. Stretch the story much longer and our listeners will be pressing us to get to the point ('Did you meet him or not?'). Few of us could keep an audience engaged for seven or eight hours, the time it takes to read a typical novel aloud. We don't know how to: we don't even have the experience of trying to.

A novel as a project

A novel, unlike that story in a bar or a two-thousand-word essay, is a substantial project, sometimes many years of work, that requires, as well as literacy, an ability to structure a complex story. In every field, from the technical to the social to the artistic, we've learned that big projects require organisation and discipline: establishing an overall shape before tackling the details, breaking the work into stages, applying different skills at different times. A building is an obvious example, but so is a song: concept, melody, rhythms, harmonies, lyrics, rewriting, arrangement, performance, perhaps recording and mixing.

This book could have been titled *What They Don't Teach You in Writing School*, because my focus is on the writing process as a whole, in particular the development of a structure and outline, rather than the shimmering sentences. But a good deal of what we're going to cover I did learn at writing school—*screenwriting* school. There, the course reflected industry philosophy and practice: story was all-important, and structure was its underpinning. Get the shape right and the details could follow.

And because screenwriting (and filmmaking in general) is a collaborative activity, there was an emphasis on process, outputs and terms to describe them. Screenwriters have to be able to communicate what they're doing, what they're going to deliver, and when. They need to be able to articulate the problems they require help with and the issues they see with others' work. When the producer wants to know how the work is progressing, 'waiting for the blood drops to form' isn't going to cut it.

I draw heavily on my screenwriting studies and experience in my novel writing, particularly in the earlier stages of outlining stories and characters.

This book treats the process of writing a novel as a *project* and presents a staged approach. Neither the stages nor the steps within them are set in stone; I encourage you to modify them in the light of your own preferences and experience, and to incorporate ideas from others.

There's plenty of advice out there about every aspect of the craft, from what you should do on waking up to whether to use the Oxford comma. What this book does is to provide a home—a context—for those tips and tutorials, and the things you've learned from practice. You should be able to find a place for any of them in one of the stages of the writing process. Once you start thinking of your work as a project, you'll likely treat related tasks, such as getting feedback on your draft, as sub-projects, and take an organised approach to them as well.

Does the process work? Is it a recipe for a bestseller? You know the answer to the second question. The success of your novel or memoir will depend on the strength of the concept, the quality of the story, your writing and, doubtless, a dose of luck. My goal is to give you a plan for writing the best book you're capable of, to the limits of your power to imagine story, your proficiency with language and the personal experience you are able to draw upon. I want to ensure that every time you sit down to work, you'll know what you need to do and will be confident that you can do it. And that, by the end of each day, you will have made visible progress toward a finished manuscript.

There's nothing radical about the process: what's important is that we are articulating it—making explicit things that otherwise happen in the writer's head—and applying it to an activity that is traditionally less organised.

Even pantsers break their work into stages, at least to some extent. With few exceptions, if their writing is to be published, they are obliged to have it edited and proofread—typically in several passes—and the profuse thanks to editors that appear in acknowledgments sections suggest that they recognise this as a good thing.

The process brings together my novel-writing and screenwriting studies, my research in design theory, and my experience writing six successful novels, starting as a midlife career-changer with no experience writing fiction. It also draws upon what I've learned from mentoring aspiring and published novelists. Notably, the only times we've failed to get a manuscript completed is when the writer has been determined not to let go of the pantser approach.

Although I present it as ten stages (Part II of this book), you can think of it as three high-level phases: planning, drafting and rewriting (which includes editing).

Basic principles

Before I outline the process in more detail, I'm going to set down eight principles that have guided it. Feel free to take issue with any of them: it's more important to know where you're coming from than to agree with me. If at any time you are unsure of how to apply the process to a particular situation, I suggest you refer back to these principles, in their original form or as modified by your own thinking.

1. Writing is a craft that can be learned—and taught. Every writer has weaknesses that can be addressed and strengths that can be enhanced.

2. Concentrate on one thing at a time. You have to create a concept, story, characters and, of course, prose. Each of these aspects is challenging; each of them matters; each deserves your best effort. The essence of a staged approach is to separate them (and indeed break them down even further), so you can focus your energy and creativity on each in its turn.

3. Make your work explicit. You're a writer, so write things down, rather than letting them float in your head, where they can escape critical review—or escape altogether.

4. Manage your creativity. Recognise that creativity can be summoned, encouraged and amplified, and that certain work practices can support it. Your subconscious mind is a great collaborator, and you need to give it a chance to contribute.

5. Get it done, then get it right. As Hemingway put it, 'The

first draft of anything is shit.' A key word here is anything. It's not just prose that improves with rewriting: story ideas, characters, every component of a novel will benefit from reworking. Embrace this maxim as you work: the first attempt won't be perfect, so don't tie yourself in knots trying to make it so. Get something down, knowing you'll come back and improve it. Your capability is not defined by the quality of your first effort but by how far you can take it, in as many passes (iterations) as you need.

6. The process is mostly top-down, but not rigidly so. Overall, we start with the big picture and add detail, from concept to outline to proofread prose. But if a brilliant line of dialogue occurs to us in the planning stage, or the writing seems to be leading somewhere different from what we planned, we can make a note for a later stage or go back and revisit our earlier work.

7. Decisions are crucial to stories. They drive plot and reveal character. Big decisions are often the foundation of your story, and the smaller decisions are the natural way of showing us the characters, setting up later action and keeping the story believable.

8. Think in scenes. Novelists are constantly told: 'show, don't tell'. Screenwriters, broadly speaking, don't have a choice, because movies and television are all about showing. Of course, you can and will have passages of exposition, description, reflection and summary, but if your book is based largely on action and dialogue happening in real time, as they might appear on the screen, it's likely to be more compelling to the general reader.

How this book is organised

This book is in two parts. The first describes ideas and techniques that are relevant throughout the writing process. The second takes you step by step through the stages, from concept to edited book.

In Part II, I use *The Rosie Result* as a case study. I chose one of my own novels because I wanted to be able to describe—rather than guess—how it was written, and selected *The Rosie Result* because it used the most evolved version of the process I'm describing here.

It's the third in a series, so I was writing with some characters already established. Accordingly, in the chapter on characters and in a few other places where *The Rosie Result* doesn't work so well to illustrate a point, or if I've wanted further examples, I've cited some of my other novels, in particular *The Best of Adam Sharp*.

I strongly recommend you read *The Rosie Result*, at least, before proceeding past this chapter. If you plan to read any of the others, best to do it now, as there are plenty of spoilers here. You'll also get a sense of the kind of books I write—and whether I'm someone you want to take advice from.

Here's an overview of what we'll cover.

Part I: Preparation

1. This chapter. The rationale and principles.

2. Being a Writer. Organising your work and life.
   Dealing with predictable crises.

3. Creativity. Principles and techniques for all stages of
   the writing process.

4. Structure. An overview of story structure and its
   components. A closer look at the popular three-act
   structure.

Part II: Process

5. Concept. Developing a concept and premise.

6. Synopsis—Plot. Producing a basic outline of the story.

7. Synopsis—Characters and Character. Fleshing out the characters in the synopsis. Developing character profiles and arcs.

8. Brainstorming the Story. Generating ideas and story beats (plot events, decisions, discoveries) without locking down their sequence. Plus some guidance on research.

9. Organising the Story. Putting the story beats in sequence to produce an outline.

10. Reviewing the Outline. Refining the story before you start writing.

11. First Draft—Process. How to go about drafting—including the daily routine.

12. First Draft—Content. My tips on writing.

13. Rewriting. Refining the draft through multiple passes.

14. Working with Your Editor. Dealing with feedback once your manuscript has been accepted for publication.

Each of the stages requires different kinds of creative thinking and has its own challenges and pleasures. But there is some repetition as we move from the big picture to detail. A story element created in the Brainstorming stage will be looked at again as you develop and review the outline, and again as you draft and rewrite—in line with the principle of revisiting and refining.

I recommend that you use this book to guide you through a real project rather than just reading it for information. The same applies if you enrol in a class: have a project in mind. That way, you can relate what you are learning to your work in progress. It will make the material more real, and you'll be moving your project forward. (*The Rosie Project* was my 'real project' over six years of writing studies; it changed enormously as my skills improved, but at the end I had a publishable novel.)

How long will it take?

How long is it going to take to complete your book? Of course, it depends—on your experience, the time you have available and how much of the story is already in your head. But I can give you a sense of the relative times for each stage and the total effort, which you'll have to fit around the rest of your life.

On the next page is my timeline for *The Rosie Result*. The activities marked with an asterisk happened in the background, while I was focused on other work: my concept brewed for a long time before I committed to it; the brainstorming was done rather haphazardly, while I was editing my previous novel; and for about a third of the editing process, the manuscript was in my editor's hands. The time from concept to submitted manuscript—probably the most meaningful metric—was forty-seven weeks. From an idea to a submitted novel in just under a year.

Circumstances vary from book to book. In this case, I had a stretch of dedicated time and a deadline for the rewriting, so it went a bit faster than usual. I was using some characters from my previous novels in the series, but still had to create their arcs for this story.

Devoting more effort to these stages is going to give you a better book. In Donna Tartt's words: 'There's a sense of richness when

Timeline for *The Rosie Result*

CONCEPT – 2 YEARS *

SYNOPSIS, INCLUDING CHARACTER ARCS – 4 WEEKS

BRAINSTORMING THE STORY – 21 WEEKS *

FROM CONCEPT
TO SUBMITTED
MANUSCRIPT
IN 47 WEEKS

ORGANISING THE STORY – 3 WEEKS
REVIEWING THE OUTLINE – 2 WEEKS

FIRST DRAFT (AVERAGE 1300 WORDS PER DAY) – 10 WEEKS

REWRITING – 7 WEEKS

EDITING WITH PUBLISHER – 26 WEEKS *

* Work happening in background

you spend a certain amount of time with characters. It's impossible to fake. There's a depth that you can't get any other way.' But that sort of deliberate, directed work is different from staring at a screen. Especially if it's your first novel, getting to a completed draft is a milestone, confirmation that you can do it. After that, you can spend as long as you like rewriting, confident that you have that foundation. As you become experienced, your trust in the process will grow, and you'll have that feeling all the way (except on the occasional bad day!).

Suppose you're not a full-time writer, but have a concept in mind and can set aside an hour per day plus half an hour of creative-thinking time, which you may be able to do while exercising, commuting or walking the dog. You've had practice writing shorter pieces and perhaps attempted a long-form work (successfully or otherwise).

Your plan from concept to a good draft, including several rewriting passes, could look something like the timeline on the following page—a full draft in eighteen months.

In the next chapter, I'm going to encourage you to keep a diary. It should, among other things, record you how much time you actually take for each stage, your daily word count and the time for each rewriting pass through the manuscript. When you plan your next book (and even as you look ahead in the drafting and rewriting stages of the current one) you can draw on that experience.

If you can devote more time to your writing, you can tighten the schedule, but the gain will be mainly in drafting and rewriting. The earlier stages need a lot of creative-thinking time, and it's unlikely—unless you're writing to a strict formula and experienced in doing so—that you'll get it done in much under a year.

That may seem like a long time if you haven't tackled a novel or novel-length work before. If you have, it may seem hopelessly optimistic. The most uncertain number is likely to be the time needed

From concept to good draft:
An hour's writing per day

18 MONTHS

SYNOPSIS, INCLUDING CHARACTER ARCS – 4 WEEKS

BRAINSTORMING THE STORY – 16 WEEKS

ORGANISING THE STORY – 4 WEEKS

REVIEWING THE OUTLINE – 4 WEEKS

FIRST DRAFT (AVERAGE 400 WORDS PER DAY) – 30 WEEKS

REWRITING – 20 WEEKS

for rewriting—but once you get to it, you'll be working with a full manuscript and the fear of non-completion should be well behind you.

If you can find the daily time, the task is not onerous. In the Brainstorming stage, you only need to come up with two story beats every day. Some days, you'll wake up in the morning with a scene in your head. While you're in the shower, you'll think of two beats to set it up and another to show the consequences. Two days' work done, and you haven't even started the clock. (Of course, you won't stop there: you'll take full advantage of that creative surge to get as much done as you can, knowing there will be tough days too.)

The daily word target in the drafting stage may look ambitious, especially if you've been a pantser, but it won't feel so daunting once you've done the planning and know what you're going to write. Don't forget, you're just getting that first draft down, not aiming for perfection. And if you can find additional time when you're on a roll, you can have some extra-productive days.

In that sense, writing a novel—even a novel that tells a coherent story—is easy. But its quality will depend on what you bring to each stage of the work. The process can provide guidance, but your knowledge of the domain you're writing in, your powers of observation and your ability to craft a good sentence (all of which can be improved, and which are only touched on in this book) will play a big role in the quality of the final manuscript.

Tailoring the process

How closely do you need to adhere to the process? Not closely at all, but it's not a bad place to start. The biggest benefits come just from having a process, giving you the confidence of knowing what you're doing, what you've achieved so far and where you're going.

As you apply it to your work-in-progress, you may find that you need to go back to an earlier stage: perhaps, as you draft, you realise that a plot line isn't working and you need to revise the outline. I flag the most common cases in the discussion of the stages.

With experience, you will likely want to change the process to suit your own needs and the kind of book you want to write. You don't have to drink coffee in the morning to get started; you may not like my technique for interrogating characters' decisions; if you disagree with the 'show, don't tell' maxim, then your outline may be built around telling rather than showing.

When my partner, Anne Buist, and I set out to co-write *Two Steps Forward* in alternating chapters, we had to design a process that would ensure our individual contributions fitted together. We ended up with a joint planning process, then a routine of passing chapters to each other for review as soon as we wrote them, then taking turns for whole-of-manuscript rewrites. When we decided to write a single-voice novel, Anne did the first draft while I followed up doing the rewriting (except when we swapped roles!). A quite different process, tailored to the circumstances—but without one, it would have been impossible to work together.

You can choose to spend more or less time than I recommend on individual stages. As a general rule, if you skimp on one stage, you'll pay for it later. If the outline has holes, drafting will be more difficult. If the draft is written carelessly, you'll spend more time editing.

If you use what's here as a starting point, you'll be making these choices consciously, aware of what you're keeping or throwing away and why. And you'll be clear on what impact it will have on your book. You'll know what you're doing.

I've written this book with novelists in mind, but the process is suitable for memoir, biography or other non-fiction stories. Besides novels and screenplays, my own writing includes short stories, a novella, a professional 'how to' book on database specification, a more academic book based on my PhD (design and creativity in a technical field), the PhD thesis itself, study materials for industry and academic courses in information-systems planning, and a collection of recipes narrated by my fictional character Don Tillman. All of them benefited from the broad process and many of the techniques described here.

What about being an artist?

It should be clear by now that this process, or at least that part of it that precedes the first draft, is not for pantser purists, and you may be reluctant to let go of the romance—and, to be fair, the results achieved by authors such as Stephen King and Zadie Smith,[1] who identify as pantsers. If you're one of those authors, and are getting the sales, accolades and personal satisfaction that you want from writing, I'm not going to argue that you should change your ways. But I'm guessing that you wouldn't be reading this book.

If you want to be seen as a stereotypical artist, then talking about 'working top-down' and 'iterative development' is not going to help: 'You make it sound like computer programming,' I've been told. That's hardly surprising. I used to be in information technology, and it's natural for me to approach a task methodically. If you've worked in any vocation that undertakes big projects, there will be much here that is familiar.

If you're a pantser who wants to try another way, you don't have to throw away the work you've done already. It's likely that much

---

[1]   Smith's discussion of Macro Planners and Micro Managers in *Changing My Mind: Occasional Essays* (2009) provides a strong personal take on the pantser approach.

of it will fit into the bigger picture as you develop it. Conversely, if you want to try pantsing, feel free: you can relinquish control, and take it back again any time you like. In either case, you don't have to become a different person: pantsing is a choice, not an identity.

If you confess to following a discipline, you'll inevitably be accused of being a slave to it. So, let me be clear: you are free at any time— not just in the planning stage—to break the rules, to deviate from my process or your plan, to ignore anything I say about structure, character and grammar if you believe it will lead to a better book. And to backtrack to what you had before if it doesn't work out.

The process is a starting point, a safety net, a fallback position if needed. For every guideline in this book, you will find an author who has broken it to brilliant effect. I'm only repeating the old adage: you need to know the rules before you can break them.

If, as you write, you change your mind about the direction of the story, go for it. If it works out, then you can revise the plan, looking for inconsistencies and opportunities to better set up the new work or play off it in other parts of the novel. In this way, your plan supports your creativity, letting you see and experiment with your choices.

And if you wake from a dream with a story fully formed, get it down, and don't answer the door (or look at your phone) until you're finished.

You're under no obligation to share your working methods, plans, drafts or character sketches with anyone. 'My drawings, never,' said Paul Gauguin to a critic who asked to see his preliminary sketches, though (as I discuss in the next chapter) I'd encourage you to develop a trusted circle of fellow writers.

As a storyteller, you have my permission to lie, as I'm sure some ostensible pantsers do. When they describe long periods of 'nothing' before they write the first word, I suspect a lack of self-awareness.

I'd bet that what is actually going on in their heads—consciously or otherwise—is a lot like planning.

Don't forget that the stereotypical artist is a *starving* artist and that 'flying by the seat of your pants' is an expression more often applied to the amateur than the pro. And don't let anyone tell you that by following a process you will be limiting yourself or your work. At every stage you will experience the fruits and joys of creativity—no less so than the pantser, and, I would argue, to better effect.

Finally, know that you're in good company. Van Gogh sketched *The Starry Night* before he put oil on canvas. Leonard Cohen filled an exercise book with draft verses for 'Hallelujah' before selecting the final seven. A web search will give you Sylvia Plath's handwritten outline for *The Bell Jar* and J. K. Rowling's for *Harry Potter and the Order of the Phoenix*.

Who cares? Only those of us who create, or study creativity. The rest of the world will rightly judge our paintings or music or novels on their merits, rather than the process by which they were created.

2
Being a Writer

I'm sometimes asked: what did you bring to writing from your previous jobs? A full answer takes a long time, because so much of what we learn in work and life is transferable to writing, both as subject matter and as contributions to the myriad skills required to write a novel: from understanding interpersonal dynamics to keeping track of computer files.

But let's get one thing out of the way. I've been told innumerable times that writing is a business. As a long-time CEO and business consultant, I disagree. Little of what I learned in business or my MBA had direct relevance to my writing. If you're going to self-publish, that's a different matter. But writing, per se, is more of a profession, a vocation or a hobby, all of which, incidentally, require theory, practice and discipline.

Writing is a business encourages writers to spend time marketing when they could be writing. And for many writers inexperienced in the field, marketing translates into social-media activity. Which has the serious drawback of being addictive and fun.

When Bill Gates, who had about thirty million followers at the

eeted praise for one of my books, I was suitably pleased, but
k didn't move one jot in the Amazon rankings. (A mention
on national television sends it flying upward.) Those of us with
more modest followings than Mr Gates, spruiking our own wares,
can't expect to improve on that. When you're posting on Facebook,
don't kid yourself that you're doing anything much for your book.
My advice on marketing to almost any writer is *use the time to write
a better book*.

There's another way that writing, for most of us, is not a business.
The financial viability of what we do is typically less important to
us than writing what we want to write. Notoriously—and surely in
part because of this attitude—most writers do not make a living from
their royalties, though quite a few manage to bridge the gap with
related work such as teaching, journalism and public appearances.
Writers occasionally observe, 'If I looked at which books had the
biggest sales and targeted that market, putting aside my own literary
ambitions, I could make a bomb.' Perhaps. And then they'd genuinely
be treating writing as a business.

Becoming a professional writer

Recognising that writing is more of a profession than a business was
not the most useful lesson from my earlier life. More important was
knowing how much time and what kind of effort it takes to become
an expert at something.

Imagine your ambition is to be an accountant or electrician or
neurosurgeon. You probably have an idea of how much study and
practice would be required. You should expect to put in a similar
amount of work to become a writer. And if the comparison with
neurosurgeons seems a stretch, consider that there are more people
making a living as neurosurgeons than as novelists. And far more

people trying to be novelists than to be neurosurgeons.

I'm not saying anything startling—it's in the same vein as the oft-quoted metric of ten thousand hours being the amount of practice required to achieve proficiency. If you want to perform at a professional level, you're going to have to work at it, even if it's something that 'we all do', like cooking or singing.

When I was studying writing, I saw few of my fellow students putting in that level of effort. Many had good reasons—a day job, family responsibilities, disabilities. Some thought their talent would be sufficient. And some just didn't think it was going to be all that hard. The bottom line was, they didn't study and practise as hard or in as disciplined a manner as students of more conventional professions.

There will always be the exception: the writer who bursts onto the scene with (supposedly) no preparation and the novel that breaks the rules but achieves massive success. The media love these stories. But I wouldn't bet your dream on their veracity or on being blessed with the amount of luck that may have accompanied them.

So, while it's true that most aspiring novelists don't make it, a significant percentage of them have not done what it takes to do so. As you do the hard yards, you can take some comfort from this. My fellow writing students who did put in the effort—and finished a manuscript—had a remarkable success rate, at least to the point of getting published.

One of them was my friend Tania Chandler. She had young children, was running a home-based childcare business, making handicrafts to sell at the local market and getting some freelance editing work. Her days were already full. So, she would get up at 5 a.m., seven days a week, and work for two hours on her writing. That was on top of attending evening classes. She did it for three years before her first novel was accepted for publication. She's still doing those two hours of early-morning work, but she's now had three novels published and her day job is as a writing teacher.

Anne, my partner in writing and life, had always wanted to be a novelist, but family pressure and financial prudence led her into a medical career. When she decided to revisit writing, she committed to producing a page every evening—and completed two manuscripts in three years. Though she secured an agent, neither novel found a publisher and she put her dream aside for twenty years. Then, 'for fun', she wrote an erotic novel that was picked up by a specialist publisher. She wrote nine more under a pseudonym: practice for story, prose and working with an editor, while picking my brains for what I was learning at writing school. When she returned to the mainstream, with the experience of twelve completed books, her first crime thriller was accepted, and she's had four published since.

And me. *The Rosie Project* was characterised as an overnight success. But I was working from a screenplay that had taken me five years to develop. During that period, the only television I watched was for screenwriting study (quite different from crashing on the sofa with a beer). I produced ten short films, wrote several short plays and had half a dozen short stories published. Not because I wanted to be the teachers' favourite but because I knew that without the effort, I wasn't going to make it.

So, it's about putting in the hours—quality hours. Persisting and progressing. The good news is that many of those hours can go directly into working on a novel: you can be making something while you're learning.

Writing life and habits

If you want more advice about how to live and work as a writer, from what exercise to do when you wake up to the last thing you should think about before falling asleep, there's plenty of it around. By all means try it out (perhaps after checking against the principles outlined in Chapter 1), but after you've been doing it for a while, take time to review and make an honest assessment of whether it works for you.

Donald Schön coined the term 'reflective practitioner' for someone who is conscious of what they're doing and what results they're getting, reflects on them, and modifies their behaviour accordingly. If something is working well, figure out why and do more of it; if it's not working, figure out why and try something else. Trust your instincts, but try to understand what has triggered them. As the saying goes, that reflection is the difference between ten years of experience and one year of experience ten times.

More broadly, you need to be aware of your goals and conscious of your strengths and weaknesses, and work accordingly to become the writer you want to be. Most budding writers I've known have a simple goal—to be published. It's not a bad goal, but it's not the only one. A completed manuscript is a significant achievement in itself. A self-published family history or memoir might have only a small audience but be hugely important to that audience. You could be aiming for critical acclaim, or sales, or to change attitudes.

Over time, you may revisit your goals, but you can only measure success against what you've set out to do. If your ambition is to top the bestseller lists, don't complain if you don't win the Pulitzer.

Personally, my greatest satisfaction comes from hearing that something I wrote has landed at the right time in a reader's life to make a difference for them. But what actually drives me to write is the prospect of creating something that I'm pleased with, proud of and sometimes even surprised by.

You'll need to come back to those reasons for writing—for being a writer—when the enthusiasm flags, the day job is consuming all your energy and the accolades you'd hoped for haven't come. You should remind yourself at such times that you're doing this, at least at some level, for fulfilment. If your writing work takes a toll on your wellbeing, you'll be undermining that most basic of goals, and likely compromising your ability to write: a potentially vicious circle. Writing is often lonely, and it's easy to let mental and physical health slide. I try to take an attitude of keeping myself in shape for the work I'm doing.

In the next chapter, I suggest that creative thinking can be combined with physical exercise: fitting writing into your life can be an opportunity to take a look at other aspects of your routine and lifestyle.

Take pleasure in your writing and forgive yourself if you don't hit your day's target. I'm a fan of the non-zero-day idea: if you get to the end of a day and have done something, no matter how small, to progress your work, pat yourself on the back. Despite all the things that get in the way of your writing, you're moving forward. And if not, forgive yourself. You can't change the past. Tomorrow is another day.

In the context of that broad advice, here are my takes on some of the questions most often asked about the writing life, plus a few additional suggestions.

Possibly the advice most frequently offered to writers is *write every day*. It's pantser advice: 'Just keep the draft moving.' In contrast, the approach I'm describing calls for different mindsets and actions at different stages, only some of which are about getting words on the page.

More than once, I've devoted a whole day to a single sentence— without writing anything down. I remember walking around

Melbourne's inner suburbs, chewing over the opening sentence for *The Rosie Project*—and finally coming up with something that I didn't use and have long since forgotten. The final answer popped into my head a few days later, as often happens when you're working on a problem: as we'll discuss in the next chapter, creativity theory recognises that hard work often needs an incubation period before it pays off. But I counted that day well spent, as forward motion on my novel-in-progress.

In the planning stages, you won't be writing as such—unless you count short notes on cards as you plan the story. Sometimes you'll be researching. It's a moot point whether editing counts as 'writing'. You may need to take time out to solve a problem. Sometimes, like me, you'll just be walking around, thinking.

But the spirit behind *write every day* is sound. If you want to succeed as a writer, you need to keep at it: doing *something* to move the project forward, continuing to develop as a writer, avoiding 'zero days'. (Unless, of course, you don't want to work a seven-day week. It's unlikely you'll get rusty if you take weekends off. The work will just go a little more slowly and your family may thank you.)

If you want to keep your writing muscles toned and have the time to do it during the planning and editing phases, then by all means work on some other projects—perhaps short stories or non-fiction pieces. But it's not essential for everyone. I do fit in some other writing at these times, but I don't make the *write every day* commitment.

I won't try to teach you about time management. There's plenty available on the subject, and you've likely settled on your own approach and habits. All I will say is that you should give your writing an appropriate level of priority: we're back to 'Imagine you're studying to be a neurosurgeon.'

Hemingway said that he'd stop each day while he still had

something to write, so he'd be able to pick up there the next day. More pantser advice! If you have a plan, you'll know where to start, every day. If you're inspired and / or on a roll (and this applies to any stage of the process, not just drafting, and even to other projects or phases you weren't planning to work on right now), keep going until the adrenaline runs out. Don't deny the muse, and don't rely on her being there tomorrow. I'm fortunate to have a partner who is also a writer. If one of us hits a hot streak, the other lets them go, even if that means taking over the dinner preparation. If we're both in that place, we'll be ordering pizza.

Keep a diary. At a minimum, record your daily progress—two new cards, 750 words written, a chapter edited. Making that entry closes off your writing day with an acknowledgment to yourself that you've made progress—or, occasionally, that you've stalled and need to do something about it. If you're feeling discouraged or negative about the book, write that down too. Later, you'll have evidence that you overcame those doubts.

Everyone will tell you that writers need to read. You do, absolutely. But reading will not, of itself, teach you to write, any more than listening to Jimi Hendrix will make you a guitar player. As Stephen King says, 'If you want to be a writer, you must do two things above all others: read a lot *and write a lot*.' (The italics are mine.)

For a writer, reading becomes different—or it should. The quality of what you read will set the limits of your own writing. And you need to read *critically*, asking how the author is achieving (or not achieving) the desired effect. You're crying or laughing or scared out of your wits—how did they do that? You're bored, skipping paragraphs. What is it about the writing that's saying, 'Ignore me'? After you finished, what passages, what scenes, what writing stayed with you? Why those? The book has been a bestseller or a critical success—what is it that resonated with the public or the critics?

While I'm in the drafting phase of a novel, I don't read any more than I have to (for book endorsements, mentoring, critiquing friends' writing—that one comes with the territory). First, it takes up time and concentration, and I want to move fast without distractions or excuses for not writing. Second, I'm likely to be pulled into the author's style, which may interfere with my own. Third, I'm intimidated: whatever I'm reading is likely to be much better than my unedited draft and that's discouraging, emotionally if not intellectually.

These are personal choices, and you may feel differently. But there will be time to read while you're planning the next novel or editing the current one.

If you can, enrol in a writing class. For me, this was a no-brainer: it's the neurosurgeon analogy again, though publishers won't be interested in your qualifications—only what they enable you to create. But if you want to be good at something, you learn the theory, practise, get feedback and mentoring from the pros, and find out about the profession and industry you hope to join. Feedback, in particular, is vital. Without it, you risk turning your mistakes into habits, like a golfer who plays round after round with a faulty swing.

It's possible to chase all of this knowledge independently, but a course packages it up and makes you do the exercises, whether you want to or not. Courses aren't perfect—if they were, I wouldn't have written this book—but they'll do more than I can to improve your prose.

The most common argument I hear against courses is that 'writing can't be taught'. I find that statement extraordinary, and counter to what we know about almost every other skill. At the extremes, there are doubtless some people who don't have it in them to write a coherent novel, and some who can write a work of genius without any tuition: geniuses, by definition. But in between—and even at those edges, I'd argue—are the people whose writing can be improved. Often from unpublishable to publishable.

When I was a writing student, I saw almost all of my classmates become better at writing. Even the most talented had weaknesses: the poetic writer who struggled with story; the brilliant plotter whose characters were unconvincing; the master of the one-liner whose wittiness distracted from the story. In my case, the prescribed work forced me to explore subjects and styles I would not otherwise have tried, and my writing was better for it.

As an older person returning to study, about to commit to many hours of work that I could otherwise have devoted directly to my writing project, I found it crucial to bring the right mindset. The key (as I've suggested with reading this book) was having a project to apply my learning to. It kept me interested, digging for things I could use—*my* responsibility, not the teachers'—and I left almost every class feeling I'd made progress.

Regardless of whether you enrol in formal study, I recommend learning some theory, if only so you know the language of your craft. Understanding the difference between scene and summary, third-person omniscient and unreliable-first-person narrator, pluperfect and simple past will not only help you communicate with your editor, but also enable you to articulate your ideas and problems.

There's an enormous amount of writing about writing, as well as short courses, seminars and podcasts. Try to make time to take some in: it makes sense to choose material that relates to the current phase of your project or the issue that's giving you difficulty.

I also suggest you join a writers' group, ideally of people at a similar stage of development to you, particularly if you don't have the opportunity to spend time with other writers in a formal course.

A writers' group gives you the opportunity to review others' work and to have your own scrutinised. It's one thing to read a fully edited book, another to read someone's manuscript in progress. You'll see mistakes that wouldn't get past an editor, and learn to identify them, name them and not make them yourself. You'll see how a manuscript improves from first to final draft. As with a writing course, you'll get used to taking on board sometimes confronting feedback on your own work.

A writers' group can be the beginning of a network that may help you to find an editor, agent or publisher, and generally to navigate the system. Your fellow writers will understand—likely more than your loved ones—the triumphs and disappointments of writing, and offer support. The group may meet in person, in online sessions or through social media. You'll likely find yourself communicating mainly with a few members whose interests and career stages are similar to yours.

A warning: it's one thing to give feedback to other writers, quite another to become invested in any solutions you offer. If someone has a brilliant idea for improving your novel, you want to have the option of rejecting it without any hard feelings. Or accepting it without your fellow writer expecting to be offered co-authorship. Make sure you extend the same courtesies to those whose work you review.

Dealing with rejection

Everyone will tell you that rejection comes with the territory. It's still hard to take.

When I enrolled in a screenwriting course, I was open about wanting to write a screenplay that would be made into a studio movie. It was a grand ambition: it's even tougher to get an original screenplay produced than a novel published. A couple of years into the course, the head of school took me aside. At that point I was, quite openly, doing all I could to achieve my goal, and she was worried that when I didn't make it (as was likely), I wouldn't be able to deal with the disappointment.

I appreciated the concern—there should be more heads of school like her—but was able to reassure her that I was enjoying the journey and the smaller achievements along the way: short films in festivals, plus a couple on television; a 'highly commended' in a writing competition; the joy of writing a piece I was proud of. Sitting in the audience at our city's arts centre watching the production of ten-minute play I'd written was one of the highlights of my life.[2]

I encourage you to give yourself a chance of small victories and celebrate them when they come. Short stories are a great way to practise your craft without taking too much time from the novel-in-progress. You can even use them to try out voices, characters and scenes for a novel. Similarly, you can prepare for a biography or memoir with an essay or personal piece.

Planning is not always so important for these shorter works: often you can hold the overall picture in your head. If you want to try the pantsing approach, the job is not so daunting and there's less work at risk.

Writing finished pieces will also get you into the habit of being critical about your work. I can almost guarantee that just before you submit the manuscript—whether printed or emailed—you'll glance over it and find something that can be improved. This is good practice for the final edits you'll do before submitting your longer work.

In the early days of writing *The Rosie Project*, I was unsure of

---

[2] Short and Sweet play festivals and Stringybark Stories were fine targets for—and then supporters of—my early writing.

whether I could pull off the voice of Don Tillman, my autistic[3] narrator, and how readers would respond to it and him. So I wrote a short story that not only helped me figure out Don a little more, but became my first piece of published fiction. I later wrote another in the voice of Don's buddy, Gene. My first non-Rosie novel, *The Best of Adam Sharp*, also grew out of a short story, this time about situation rather than character.

If your short stories are published or receive recognition in a competition, you are building your credentials for the time when you approach agents and publishers.

But what if they're not published? And what if they are, but your novel still doesn't find a publisher? How do you deal with it? We all know that many of the greatest books and authors have been rejected, often over and over. I recommend looking up your favourite novel online and reading the one-star reviews. Novels are a matter of taste and your work won't suit everyone. I had rejections for *The Rosie Project*. And my international publishers didn't take up some of my later books. Though I'd experienced success, it still hurt.

One thing I did that proved to be helpful was to do a mental stocktake when I did achieve my goal of publication. I said to myself, 'You've made it. Your book's going to be published—everything else is a bonus.' I've revisited that moment many times, and it's been useful in dealing with setbacks and disappointments.

Sometimes, the person doing the rejecting is you—abandoning work before anyone else has a chance to tell you to. It happens to all of us, but you have to know the difference between a temporary loss of confidence and a rational decision that the project isn't working

---

[3] I use 'identity-first' language rather than 'person-first' language when referring to autism, in line with guidelines from the autism community.

and that your effort would be better spent elsewhere. Be conscious of your own state of mind and get another trusted opinion (even if it's just talking the decision through). Put the work aside and review it again later. One of the good things about writing is that projects can be resurrected, sometimes years later.

After you've dusted yourself off and got back on the bike, take the time to reflect on what worked and what didn't and what you might use again. If you do that, you can reassure yourself that the effort was not wasted. It's practice, and you may find that parts of it find their way into later work.

For me, the best solution to rejection of any kind was to have other irons in the fire: another competition or publication for my short story, another festival for my short film, another work in progress. And that new novel that's moving inexorably toward completion.

Dealing with success

I'm not going to tell you how to spend your money when your book becomes a bestselling phenomenon, but I will say this. As you become more accomplished and established as a writer, find time to put something back, in particular to help other emerging writers. Good karma.

3
Creativity

What is a writer's most precious resource? What is it that we'd like more of to get our book finished? Those who have to fit their writing around other commitments are likely to respond, reflexively, *time*—but I'd argue that it is, in fact, creativity.

When the words are coming easily, as they sometimes do, many of us can get a thousand or more down in an hour. But few can maintain the creative energy that fuels it. During the COVID-19 lockdowns, some of my writer friends found they had time on their hands and, to their enormous frustration, were unable to translate it into productive writing. The ability to 'fill the empty space', to solve problems and, at the detailed level, to create fresh prose proved to be the real limiting factor.

This is particularly true in the earlier stages of a project, which are largely about coming up with material and working out how to turn it into a cohesive story. In planning *The Rosie Result*: 'We need a big final setback before the climax.' 'How do I get Gene back into the story?' 'What obstacles will Don face in coaching Hudson?'

We'll look at creative techniques specific to each stage in the associated chapters: brainstorming plot ideas, suppressing your inner critic when drafting, focusing on problem definition when dealing with plot issues. This chapter looks at principles applicable to the whole of the writing process—indeed, to just about any creative activity.

Harnessing your creativity

Much of the advice you'll find on creativity is personal or anecdotal: 'This worked for me so it might (or *will*) work for you.' I'll offer a twist on that, in line with the principle of being a reflective practitioner: find out what works for *you* and harness it. It's the most important step in moving from seeing creativity as unpredictable magic to an aspect of thinking that can be managed, if not always summoned at will.

Start by taking note of the circumstances in which you have your eureka moments—or at least your ideas and your solutions to problems. I've found that walking, easy exercise at the gym and cooking familiar dishes are conducive to creative thinking. So is the first drink with my partner at the end of the day. I'm not encouraging you to take up alcohol or any other drug: I'd just say, be aware of how these factors affect your creativity. (And if an honest assessment indicates that your lifestyle is hurting any aspect of your writing, you'll need to decide which is more important.)

Once you know what circumstances are conducive to the muse, you need to create them deliberately, routinely, as part of your writing day. Mine begins with either an on-foot shopping trip, a run or a workout at the gym. And at 6.30 p.m. I pour a drink for my partner (and sometime co-author) and me, and we talk about our writing problems.

This time is valuable: as much as possible, I devote it to creative thinking. I may be walking to the market, but I don't want to be trying to remember what I'm supposed to buy. If there's something else besides my writing that needs attention, I work on that too (it's taking up mind-space, so best to get it sorted).

You need to reflect deliberately on the work or problems you see in front of you, but you'll find that solutions to earlier problems you've put on hold will come to you unbidden. It's a magical feeling, and I almost never finish a walk or workout without something to make my current novel better. I consider even one idea to be a good return for my time, and of course that reinforces my commitment to the process and my confidence in it. It's enormously empowering to know that virtually every problem you'll encounter in your writing can be solved—you've always found a way through in the past, and you will again.

This is a good time to mention the habit of carrying a notebook or electronic equivalent, like a notes or voice-memo app. If you opt for the latter, it needs to be something that doesn't take time to set up. Ideas often come in a rush, and not always during time allocated for creativity. You need to get them down before they disappear (awkward if you've chosen swimming as your routine exercise). Creativity is hard work and when it produces results, you want to hold on to them. In Elizabeth Gilbert's TED Talk on creative genius, she describes the poet Ruth Stone racing through fields to get to her notebook to write out a poem when it hit her.

I go through my notes when I begin work each day and either apply the ideas to the relevant project or add them to an action list or ideas list, as appropriate.

Principles and techniques

Your exploration of the settings for creativity and how to best use them can be informed by a few established principles of creativity and design theory:

1. Routine physical activities are often conducive to creativity.

2. Focus on one problem at a time.

3. Experiment with combinations.

4. Give the subconscious a chance (allow an incubation period).

5. Solutions often create new problems.

6. You can always make it better.

7. Two heads can be better than one.

Routine physical activities

Driving, walking and, famously in the case of the ancient Greek mathematician Archimedes, taking a bath or shower: these relatively undemanding physical activities are widely recognised as fertile settings for creativity. They do need to be routine, both in the sense that you do them regularly (ideally daily, at the same time) and in not requiring much concentration. Driving in city traffic, deciphering an unfamiliar recipe or trying to beat your personal best on the track is not going to cut it.

And yes, I know that we should be concentrating when we drive, but most of us on a long commute listen to the radio or let our thoughts wander. At least thinking about writing won't take your eyes off the road.

If you don't do any of these, I suggest you take up walking or easy jogging. ('Scratch a writer and you'll find a walker,' says Tegan Bennett Daylight. 'Trust no thought arrived at sitting down,' said George Sheehan, the 'Running Doctor'.) In my experience, thirty minutes is sufficient to get my mind into the right place without too much effort and—nearly every time—make progress on whatever aspect of my writing I'm working on. Plus, you'll be doing something for your wellbeing: feeling healthy is definitely a plus in being creative, and in approaching the day's writing work.

If you do run out of creative energy as you're working, I'd suggest refuelling by repeating your creativity routine rather than staring at the screen.

Focus

One of the guiding principles of this book—and indeed much of the rationale for tackling a novel or memoir as a staged project—is to focus on one thing at a time. Psychologists talk about *cognitive load*: if your mind is doing something other than working on the task at hand, you're not getting the benefit of its full power.

So, turn off the phone and disconnect the internet. You know that, but science agrees. Music is a moot point: some people work with earphones in, others (including me and many of my vintage) do better in silence. As with all things creative, you need to find what works for you, but I'd counsel you not to be listening *intently*; choose familiar, low-key or innocuous music.

Then, do your best to break your problems down into their smallest, clearly articulated components: you want to get from 'It's all too hard' (with theatrical throwing of hands in the air) or 'I'm blocked' to something like 'I need to find a teaching moment between Don and Hudson that's more emotionally powerful than anything I've come up with so far.'

Experiment with combinations

A great source of original ideas is two or more maybe-not-so-original ideas brought together. The principle, straight out of probability theory, is that the combination of these ideas will be far less common than those ideas by themselves. How many love stories have been published? Innumerable. How many books set on the Camino de Santiago? A search on Amazon yields over a thousand results. But love stories on the Camino de Santiago? Anne's and my *Two Steps Forward* is one of (at most) a handful. We'll see more examples of this technique in the chapters on concepts and characters.

Breaking the rules

Breaking the established rules might seem like the quickest path to originality. Craft an entire novel in eight sentences; write exclusively in second-person future conditional; leave out quotation marks. Problem is, with so many books out there, it's almost certainly been done before. By itself, it's unlikely to do more than alienate readers or draw attention to your desire to be different.

If it's in service of an idea—if it helps you achieve the effect you're aiming for—that's a different matter. As with the overall process, if you know why the rules are there and why you're breaking them, you can make an informed decision.

But—the value of experimenting with combinations notwithstanding—think hard before you break more than one writing rule at a time. The result is likely to be a bridge too far for many readers.

Incubation period

I've suggested that creativity may be a scarcer resource than time, but creativity itself needs time. Researchers note the importance of an incubation period between recognising a problem and finding a solution. The period varies, but we're typically talking about at least two or three weeks. In that time, your subconscious is beavering away—and that's a wonderful thing. Your job is to give it a briefing and a flying start by working as hard as you can on the problem before setting it aside.

When the solution does come, it can be one of the most joyful aspects of writing, your subconscious delivering something way beyond what you might have come up with consciously. But take a bow—it's still you. And you'll often find that the solution draws cleverly on existing aspects of the story—sometimes even passages you've abandoned that you'll now reinstate—as though they were put there for the purpose.

In *The Rosie Project* (which began as a screenplay), Rosie is seeking her biological father. When a group of actors did a read-through, they were unanimous in telling me that the answer felt wrong: 'Gene shouldn't be her father.' I thought long and hard about how to set it up better, then put the matter aside. A couple of weeks later, a solution popped into my head: not a better set-up, but a different character. And I realised I'd already set that character up almost perfectly. The answer had been waiting in my head all along. And I had the bonus of a red herring in the form of Gene.

But what do we do while we're waiting for our subconscious to do its work? If you're a pantser, you might find yourself stopped in your tracks—*blocked*. But we planners have options. In the longest stage—the generation of story beats—sequence is not important, so while we wait for an answer to 'What crisis will befall Don and Hudson that threatens to undo all of their plans?' we can shift our attention to other aspects of the story. Likewise, in editing we can jump around. Even in drafting, having a plan allows us to skip ahead to another section.

The phenomenon of ideas emerging after an incubation period will often catch you by surprise. Out of nowhere—but typically during the time set aside for creativity—an idea related to something you were working on recently will pop up. Often, it's a way of improving a passage you've written—a new and neat detail. This happens commonly in drafting, and if you're already on a roll it can feel a bit overwhelming: an embarrassment of riches. 'I should be so lucky,' says the writer waiting for the blood drops. If it's simple, I tend to open the computer and do it right away—if not, it goes in the notebook.

Solutions create new problems—and opportunities

Not every solution is as clean as my answer to 'Who is Rosie's father?', and even in that case I had to tweak the plot to accommodate the new choice. The design theorist Bryan Lawson[4] observes that solutions to problems almost invariably create new problems of their own. So don't reject a solution just because it creates new problems—at least not without exploring solutions to those problems.

Sometimes, it does turn out that your clever idea has an impact that is incompatible with what you want to do with the book, but more often the chain of problems and solutions leads to a better outcome overall. Time and again, I've found that in solving one problem, I've fixed others, because they were in my mind as well.

The flip side is that often a solution suggests ideas for elsewhere in the story. Indeed, it's worth asking: 'What possibilities does this change open up?' In *The Rosie Result* I had the problem that Don

---

[4] If you want to learn more about creativity, and are prepared to look at the process of writing a book as an exercise in design (as I am), Lawson's *How Designers Think: The Design Process Demystified* is an interesting read.

leaving his job in genetics to care for Hudson would create financial stress. There were plenty of possible solutions, but I settled on the one with the most comedic possibilities: Don establishing his own bar. This gave me not only a bunch of scenes, but led to the idea of an autism-friendly bar. But where would he get the capital for this? That problem was solved by giving a bigger role to an existing character (Minh—Don's potential new employer in genetics), which in turn...

You can always make it better

When a solution arrives that does everything you're looking for and more, fitting in with and reinforcing work already done, and setting up possibilities you hadn't seen before, it's tempting to call it perfect. But both theory and experience teach us that any solution—from a sentence to a full manuscript—can be made better. Maybe we don't need to; maybe we've reached the point of diminishing returns; maybe it's better that the paragraph we're working on matches the quality of the rest of the book, rather than standing out for its brilliance and forcing us to improve all the rest.

We don't want to be like the aspiring author in Albert Camus' *The Plague*, working forever to create the perfect first sentence. But equally, we need to keep in mind that what we've planned and written can almost always be improved.

Indeed, there are certain points where we may want to put in a special effort to make something as good as we can. Camus' character wasn't entirely wrong: a book's opening is critical, as are the title, basic premise and ending. In these cases, after we find a solution, we can restart the process—continue to give the problem some of our creative time and let the solution evolve further (or be replaced by something dramatically different). Titles, openings and endings can be revised over and over but it's usually a big job to change the premise once you're underway. That's one reason that I let premises brew in my head for a long time before pressing 'go' on the project.

None of my books have been published with their original working title. *The Rosie Project* was at various times *The Face of God* (yep), *Natural Selection* and *The Klara Project*. *The Best of Adam Sharp*, the story of a musician who missed his big chance at love, began as *The Candle* but my subconscious managed to pull together a popular form of album title in the sixties, the theme of him becoming a better person and the opening line of Chapter 1, where he mentions Pete Best, the Beatles original drummer who also lost his big opportunity. *Two Steps Forward* began as *Walk to the Stars* and for a while was *Left Right*.

Two heads

I've left collaboration till last; it's not for everyone—perhaps only those who've felt the creative sparks flying when they're kicking an idea around with someone else or have found that sharing a plot problem with a friend led to a solution.

I've suggested you seek feedback (and the opportunity to give it yourself) by joining a course and / or a writers' group. But enlisting others in a more active creative role is a bigger step, and counter to the idea of the novelist as a solo practitioner, alone in their garret. Few novels—compared with non-fiction books—list more than one author. I'm one of those exceptions, having written two novels with my partner, so I'm perhaps more aligned with the idea than most novelists.

In screenwriting, it's all about collaboration, partly because there's often a need to generate a lot of material quite quickly—'Guys, they've commissioned a second season'—and partly because there's so much investment at stake that producers will want second and third opinions. Drafting remains largely a solo effort: it's the planning in the writers' room (which, incidentally, is seen as the core creative process) and the rewriting that involves others.

Novelists are already accustomed to collaboration in the editing phase. There's also a strong argument for getting a second or third head involved in the concept and planning stages when we're doing much the same thing as our screenwriting brethren: generating a story. I work with my partner on her novels and mine, particularly as we begin to pull ideas together into a coherent narrative (Organising the Story and Reviewing the Outline). Sometimes it's over our evening drink, just kicking around an idea or two; other times we spend many hours on a substantial part of the story. We do it because it works. There's a lot in my novels that I wouldn't have come up with alone.

You need to choose your collaborators wisely. A writing group is an obvious place to look but an enthusiastic friend or partner, who doesn't need to be a writer, is sometimes a great option. You're not looking for criticism—or even honesty—but enthusiasm and ideas: someone who can get on board with your concept and help to build it up.

Other creativity techniques

What about all the other creativity techniques: 'free writing' for an hour every morning, looking for inspiration in random words in the dictionary…there are plenty around, including some aimed specifically at writers.

As a consultant in business-process redesign, I used Edward de Bono's Six Thinking Hats technique, and have occasionally drawn on its principles in a (screen) writers' room. But, despite being very comfortable with it, I have never used it in novel writing.

If any of these approaches appeal to you or seem to be addressing a gap in your capabilities, by all means try them out. And as always, in the role of reflective practitioner, make an objective decision about whether they work for you.

On getting stuck

It's not just writer's block, which we associate with the drafting stage. At any time in the process, you can run out of ideas or solutions. For me, it happens most often when I'm brainstorming the story (not enough material) or rewriting (a problem I'm struggling to solve).

Three suggestions:

1. Don't get it right; get it done. This was the mantra that saw Joe Queenan through his low-budget movie (so memorably described in *The Unkindest Cut* that it inspired me to become a writer). Lower your standards; just get something down: a card that says 'Something bad happens to Don'; a passage that tells the story, no matter how clumsily. You can make it better later.

2. Put it aside and work on something else, to let incubation work its magic—*after giving it your best shot*.

3. Be wary of dismissing a difficult problem as the result of 'having a bad day'—or two or three. Sometimes a problem that looks like it should be easy to solve ('I know what I'm trying to say: I just can't find the right words') but is proving intractable is a symptom of something deeper ('I don't really know what I'm trying

to say'). Recognise that it may take more than a cup of espresso to solve. And remind yourself that you've always found a way through. If you stick with it, in a year's time—probably in a month's time—today's insurmountable problem will be the brilliant idea that made your novel. Or at least a distant memory.

4
Structure

Life, it's been said, is just one damn thing after another. We expect more from stories. Whether it's something intrinsic to the human psyche or just what we've become accustomed to, we want the events in stories to be connected, driven by the decisions of one or more credible characters, with rising and falling intensity, leading to a climax and resolution. Not all stories have all of these features, but they're what most readers will be expecting when they pick up your book.

Conversely…Here are a few notes I made on a manuscript sent to me for review:

What is the dramatic question here?

The protagonist is a passive victim, rather than a driver.

How does the journey to South America contribute to what comes later?

The resolution comes from nowhere—not set up.

The author pointed out that the story was based on their own life: 'These things really happened.' Unfortunately, fidelity to real life isn't enough, at least in popular fiction. Truth is indeed stranger than fiction, and the reader expects us to keep it that way!

Even if you're writing a memoir, unless you're so famous that the reader's fascination with your life trumps their desire for story, your book needs a structure that engages the reader and enables you to achieve the effects you intend.

The structure is the framework that supports the scintillating prose, keeps the reader engaged and enables you to tell a *story*: to say something beyond 'Look how beautifully I write' and 'Here are some events and observations'. In my experience, an understanding of structure is what aspiring novelists most often lack—and need most.

So, when asked to recommend a book on writing, I send aspiring novelists and memoirists to the screenwriting section of the bookshop, to Syd Field's classic *Screenplay: The Foundations of Screenwriting* or the TV producer and editor John Yorke's *Into the Woods: How Stories Work and Why We Tell Them*. Because screenwriters—and producers—are structure nuts.

Whenever we had an industry pro address our screenwriting class, they would outline their personal take on how a screenplay should be structured, beginning with the ubiquitous three-act format (we'll get to that shortly), then adding their own variations or overhauls. You'll see the same if you pick up one of the many screenwriting books that have followed Field's. Some of these are so prescriptive that they specify the page numbers in the script at which certain events ('plot points') should occur. Blake Snyder's *Save the Cat! The Last Book on Screenwriting You'll Ever Need* is a good example. Movie producers will look at a screenplay expecting to find those plot points in the right places.

Some of these books (notably *The Writer's Journey: Mythic Structure for Writers* by Christopher Vogler) flesh out their templates with ideas from Joseph Campbell's *The Hero with a Thousand Faces*, which argued that traditional stories and myths followed a Hero's Journey, a pattern of seventeen generic steps such as 'the call to adventure', 'meeting with the mentor' and the evocatively named 'belly of the whale' (Vogler's book cuts the number of steps to twelve).

How to use structure

I'm not going to ask you to wear any of those screenwriting gurus' straitjackets, but you should definitely try a couple on to see how they fit your story and what you can take from them. This chapter is in Part I because I *don't* want to prescribe how your novel should be structured. What I want is for you to be familiar with the most important elements of structure, so you can make and articulate decisions about how you shape your own story—in other words, so you know what you're doing and what you're rejecting, and have the words to talk about it.

Your book doesn't have to follow the three-act structure, but there are worse places to start. Yes, it's more 'original' to use a non-standard structure, just as it's more 'original' to write music using a scale and time signature of your own invention. The creativity researcher and Pulitzer Prize winner Douglas Hofstadter says, 'The crux of creativity lies in the ability to manufacture variations on a theme.' You need a reason—a good reason—to deviate from familiar structural conventions.

Star Wars was famously built on the Hero's Journey structure. If you're looking for something more literary, you could start with *The Road Home* by Rose Tremain, winner of the Orange Broadband Prize for Fiction in 2008, and, as an exercise, check off the steps in the

Hero's Journey. And novel after novel follows a three-act structure without feeling like a Hollywood movie.

I consciously employed the three-act structure for all but one of my novels and for my novella. (Perhaps it's no coincidence that the exception was the least commercially successful.) I routinely use the Hero's Journey for reference and inspiration without feeling any obligation to hit all seventeen beats. In *Two Steps Forward*, Anne and I overlaid two Hero's Journeys with a romantic-comedy subplot. We'll talk more about choosing a specific structure for your story in Chapter 9.

If you do it well, a book's structure will be invisible to ordinary readers—as distinct from writers like you and me, who are looking for it in the same way that a musician might analyse a bass line rather than just rocking to the song. To take our musical analogy a step further, even if our bassist had improvised their contribution, we could still notate it from the live performance or a recording: the notes and rhythms exist and can be analysed regardless of the process that created them. Similarly, books have structures, even if they arise organically rather than through intent. We can identify those structures and use them to analyse, discuss and (if the writing is our own) improve the book. So it's worth knowing about structure even if you don't want to use it as a planning tool.

The language of structure

Below I've outlined seven elements common to almost everybody's structural prescription. They give us a language for describing and comparing structures. There's no governing body for these terms: you're bound to see variations in definitions, but they're sufficient for planning and communication. In the next section, we'll see examples of their use in the three-act structure template.

1. *Story beats* (or just *beats*). These are the basic elements—the smallest components of your structure. *The school requests an autism assessment for Hudson; Don quits his job to coach Hudson; Hudson triumphs at the swimming carnival.* Templates like the Hero's Journey typically identify around five to twenty key beats, but a detailed outline for a novel could have 120 beats (fewer if you're happy to work with a rougher outline).

2. *The Inciting Incident* (or *The Call to Adventure*). Messages, murders, meetings with a prospective romantic partner— these are the events (sometimes one beat, sometimes several) that set the story in motion. *Adam gets an email from his lover of twenty years ago.* Usually, they're external, but they often require a decision—the first critical decision—on the part of the protagonist. That decision may be negotiated and agonised over: after *The Call to Adventure*, the Hero's Journey includes *Refusal of the Call* before final commitment.

3. *The Dramatic Question.* It may not be stated baldly, or tied to a particular beat, but early in the story a central question will usually emerge—and signal to the reader that the story will wend its way toward answering that question. It's frequently associated with a goal that the protagonist is seeking. *Will Adam reunite with his ex-lover? Will these two crazy kids fall in love? Whodunnit?* What's often not mentioned is that the question may change over the course of the book—though usually only once or twice. In *The Rosie Project*, the initial dramatic question is *Will Don find a partner using his quirky questionnaire?* But after he meets the patently unsuitable Rosie, those of us versed in the traditions of romantic comedy know that the question is now *Will Don and Rosie get together?*

The reader expects these dramatic questions to be
answered either at the point that they're replaced by a new
question or at the story's climax.

4. *Turning points.* These are the beats in the story that send the
    narrative off in a new direction. We've already met one: the
    inciting incident. Turning points are an important way of
    keeping the reader interested and surprised, and the term is
    usually reserved for a few (typically four or five) big moments
    in the story directly affecting the protagonist(s), rather than
    more minor setbacks and reversals: *Adam decides to leave
    his partner in the hope of reuniting with his ex-lover Angelina.*
    Sometimes turning points are events beyond the protagonist's
    control (*Zoe's husband is killed in a car accident*); sometimes
    they are decisions (*Zoe decides to walk the Camino*); often, they
    are a combination of the two—an external event followed by
    the protagonist's response.

    When the turning points are decisions made by the
    protagonist, they not only drive plot, but also position the
    protagonist as the architect rather than the victim of the story
    and help to define their character.

    At a turning point, our protagonist's goal may change
    (which will likely mean a change to the dramatic question
    too) or they may take a new approach to achieving it, typically
    after one approach has failed.

    In a standard structure, some of these turning points will,
    like the inciting incident, have their own names: first-act turning
    point, midpoint and so on. And 'point' is a little too precise. The
    change may not take place in a single moment, a single sentence,
    but may be spread out, even over a chapter or two.

5. *Acts.* The division of a story into acts comes from staged drama, where the breaks between them are marked in the script and made visible to the audience by the fall and rise of the curtain. Shakespeare followed ancient tradition in writing his plays in five acts. Broadcast television, with its episodes punctuated by commercial breaks, brought its own act structures. Streaming series have challenged those rules and established new formulas.

   In novels and movies, the readers or audience don't see a curtain rise and fall, but they are conscious that the story has moved to a different phase, possibly to a different time and place. And that, of course, is the result of a turning point doing its job of 'setting the narrative off in a new direction'. So acts and turning points are closely related.

   Acts can be seen as mini-stories in themselves, their beginnings and ends marked by turning points. If you want to see and understand the act break-up of an existing story—and I strongly recommend this as a routine exercise when reading or watching a movie—look for the big turning points and when they occur. (Our two-writer family, watching a movie at home, is liable to chorus, 'First-act turning point' and check our watches.)

6. *Climax.* As the name implies, the climax represents the highest point of the drama, which has usually been building, and makes at least a start on resolving the dramatic questions (plot and subplot). In *The Best of Adam Sharp*, this is the moment that Adam chooses between his long-term partner and his former lover (and the possibility of neither). It may take place over several beats if the drama can be sustained for that long.

7. *Denouement* (or *Coda*). The loose ends are tied up and aspects
    of the dramatic question that weren't resolved in the climax
    are answered. This part is usually short, sometimes presented
    as an epilogue, because the dramatic high point has passed,
    and we are now into 'falling action'. In the last paragraph of
    The Best of Adam Sharp, we learn that Adam and his partner
    have taken up the job she was offered in the United States,
    that he's returned to performing music, and that he never sees
    his former lover again.

The three-act structure

We can use the terms introduced in the last section to describe the
majority of story structures. Let's apply them to that most common
of novel and movie shapes, the *three-act structure*. If you understand
how this structure works, you can ring the changes yourself to create
other options: you don't need to learn a whole repertoire.

Essentially, the three-act structure divides a story into Act 1:
Set-up, Act 2: *Complications / Escalation* and Act 3: *Resolution*. Most
conventional stories could be shoe-horned into that framework.
What's more prescriptive is the (optional) guideline that the three
acts should account for, respectively, one-quarter, one-half and
one-quarter of the story.

That guideline has come from observations (largely of movies),
and a view that audiences have come to expect these proportions.
I'm not here to argue that position, but book editors seem to agree
with the screenwriting pundits. Present a set-up that's more than a
quarter of the book and a final act that's less than that, as frequently
happens, and expect to be told that the book is slow to get moving
and the ending is rushed.

A conventional three-act story looks broadly like the diagram on the next page. (I've used *The Rosie Result* as an example in the discussion that follows.)

1. *Act 1: Set-up.* Traditionally, the story begins by showing the protagonist(s) in their 'ordinary world' before the inciting incident kicks off the story. In these impatient times, we will often defer such background information until the story gets moving—or even forever—unless it's particularly engaging in its own right. When we meet someone in real life, we're seldom privy to much more than their name and occupation before we launch into conversation and, perhaps, an adventure.

    So, before the reader loses interest, the inciting incident comes along and creates a dramatic question, and typically a goal, that drives the narrative. Act 1 finishes (and Act 2 begins) with the *Act 1 Turning Point*.

    In *The Rosie Result*, I spend some time, and a couple of mini-stories, introducing the reader to Don and Hudson's ordinary world, because their way of living in and perceiving that world is unusual and hopefully interesting to readers. Hudson's ongoing difficulties at school are background to the inciting incident—the school principal's suggestion that he be assessed for autism. This comes relatively late—on page 46 of the 376-page novel—and raises the dramatic question: *Will Don (and Rosie) be able to solve Hudson's problems?* The reader may also be engaged by the associated question: *Is Hudson actually autistic?* Don and Rosie set off looking for information and solutions as Hudson's problems escalate. Comedy and drama accrue from their interactions with the system.

A conventional three-act story

INCITING INCIDENT

ACT 1: SET-UP

FIRST ACT TURNING POINT

ACT 2: ESCALATION

MIDPOINT

SECOND ACT TURNING POINT

ACT 3: RESOLUTION

CODA

The Act 1 Turning Point occurs when Don decides to quit his job and coach Hudson on 'fitting in'. The story has changed direction: we know that Don doesn't fit in too well himself, so we've set up a comedy of the blind leading the blind. Complications will surely follow, and they're the stuff of Act 2.

The turning point brings with it a refinement of our dramatic question. It's now: *Can Don succeed in coaching Hudson to fit in?* The new direction is confirmed when Rosie says, 'Something had to change. You've made the right call' on page 95. Right on quarter-time.

2. *Act 2: Complications / Escalation ('The Road of Trials').* The narrative continues and develops, driven by the dramatic question and associated goal(s). The reader expects *escalation*: the challenges and stakes getting bigger. Because Act 2 is half the book, and it can be difficult to keep the stakes escalating for so long, we often break it up with another turning point near the middle of the act (which is also the middle of the whole story). It's called, logically enough, the *Midpoint*. Typically, the dramatic question remains, but there's some change in the protagonist's approach to solving it—and the escalation starts again. You could reasonably argue that the midpoint effectively creates a four-act structure, but everybody calls it a three-act structure with midpoint.

The *Act 2 Turning Point* at the end of the act usually marks a low point in the story—sometimes called *All Is Lost*—with the hero failing to achieve their goal. This prompts another change in direction and often a change in goal, from something relatively superficial to something internal and more profound.

In *The Rosie Result*, the midpoint is when Don's coaching fails to solve Hudson's school problems, which are (of course) escalating. So Don enlists his friends to help. The goal is the same, but the method has changed. It's on page 182 (six pages short of halfway) that he announces: 'The Hudson Project would need to be outsourced.'

We hit our low point—the Act 2 Turning Point—when Hudson has been suspended from school for allegedly killing a pigeon and will not be accepted into high school unless he sees a psychologist, which he refuses to do.

On page 290, just eight pages past the three-quarter mark, Hudson announces, 'I've got this', and we move into Act 3, which will be driven by Hudson's own efforts.

3. *Act 3: Resolution.* This is the final stage of the journey to the climax, where the dramatic question (created back in Act 1 by the inciting incident, and possibly changed or refined along the way) will be answered. Again, we expect escalating stakes and even more drama than in the second act. The pace picks up. There will be gains and setbacks and perhaps a false ending—another turning point where the protagonist fails and has to pick themselves up one last time, or even succeeds then surprises us by rejecting the reward it brings so they can pursue that more significant internal goal. Then the climax, when the dramatic question is (largely) answered and the protagonist's goal is achieved—or not. A short *Coda* (*Denouement*) may tie off the loose ends.

In *The Rosie Result*, Hudson, through his own efforts, finally succeeds in fitting in and achieves his goal of acceptance into high school. This resolves the original dramatic question, but the reader has learned along the way that there's a deeper (internal) question about whether he and Don, our narrator, will come to terms with their autism.

Hudson rejects his reward: instead, he acknowledges his autism and announces he's chosen to attend a special school. The climax is in the last line of the last chapter, when Don acknowledges and accepts his own autism with the statement: 'Always a mistake to underestimate an aspie.'

An epilogue (so titled) is the coda, explaining how the outstanding issues of jobs, school and relationships are tied off.

What about subplots? Many versions of the three-act structure (*Save the Cat!* is a notable exception) don't have much to say about them. At this point, let's just note that:

1. They're not mandatory: plenty of fine stories have a subplot or subplots and plenty don't.

2. They typically start late in the first act or early in the second, once the main story is established, or may be 'left over' from the beginning when the main story shifts direction.

3. As stories in themselves, they follow a similar arc of set-up, complication / escalation and resolution.

4. They are usually linked to the main story through common characters, intersections with the main plot, and / or similar themes—often all three.

5. We usually aim to resolve them at or close to the climax of the main story.

In *The Rosie Result*, we have several subplots unfolding in parallel with Hudson's journey, using characters from the main story, interweaving with the main plot and touching on issues of difference and acceptance. Rosie struggles with a misogynist boss, Don establishes an autism-friendly bar and Hudson's friend Blanche rebels against her family's refusal to countenance mainstream medical support for her albinism.

Then, there are *runners*—recurring events or an ongoing minor story, often comedic—such as Don repeatedly causing damage to his father-in-law's Porsche.

Beyond the three-act structure

Not all stories fit comfortably into three acts and not all writers want to be bound by that structure. As noted, real life doesn't play out in three acts, or according to any other storytelling template. Stakes and tension don't escalate steadily, if at all. Dramatic questions may never be resolved and loose ends may stay loose.

If you're writing a memoir or biography, you need to be conscious that it may not fit into a conventional structure, and that readers, accustomed to stories being told in a predictable way, may be less engaged. You can often at least partially solve the problem by judicious choice of start and endpoints, of what you choose to include and the order in which you tell the story.

If your memoir or biography—or indeed novel concept—doesn't fit a three-act structure, you may be able to break it into two or more stories that do: 'The young hoodlum'; 'The rock-star years: rise to the top'; 'Love and tragedy'.

Abandoning the three-act structure altogether, you can write a series of loosely connected vignettes, as in David Sedaris's collections or Bob Dylan's *Chronicles*. Anne and I are consciously following the structure of a TV series for a novel set in a psychiatric ward. If you're telling the story of a disordered life, with memories missing or contradictory, you might adopt a structure that reflects this, as in Lidia Yuknavitch's *The Chronology of Water* or Sarah Krasnostein's *The Trauma Cleaner*.

If you choose an unconventional path, you may want to signal it to the reader—for example, by dividing the book explicitly into parts. Sequence almost always matters: you may not be telling a story chronologically, but you can do a lot to manage the reader's comprehension and emotional arc.

I'd strongly counsel you to read a few well-regarded contemporary memoirs and biographies, taking note of their structures and how well they work. One of them or a combination is likely to be what you need for your project.

Whatever you choose, make your structure explicit to yourself so you know what you're doing and what choices you're making.

That should be enough information about structure for you to make sense of the rest of this book, and to write your novel or memoir. But if you're interested (and I strongly encourage you to be), you can find any number of books and articles, beyond those mentioned above, which will add structural tools and templates to your storytelling armoury.

If you've chosen to write in a genre such as crime, romance or thriller, you should familiarise yourself with the established structure(s) for that genre, which you may then follow or transgress—the important thing is to understand which of those you're doing. *The Seven Basic Plots* by Christopher Booker looks not only at the structure but at the history and psychological underpinning of established story types. *Story* by Robert McKee is a substantial book aimed at screenwriters but almost certain to provide ideas for your novel.

When I was writing *The Rosie Project*, a romantic comedy (historically more of a movie genre than a novel genre), I read Billy Mernit's *Writing the Romantic Comedy* and attended a couple of romantic-comedy screenwriting seminars, learning the specialist structural variants, such as the *meet-cute* as inciting incident and *boy loses girl* as the *all is lost* second-act turning point. With those shapes and conventions in mind, I watched a slew of movies (and read a couple of novels), checking it all off.

Then, knowing all that, I could write my novel in my own way.

PART II
Process

5
Concept

At the end of this stage, you'll have:

1. A concise statement of what your novel or memoir is about

2. An initial list of ideas for your story.

'Where do you get your ideas?' Every author has been asked that question, as if it's the most important—almost the only—aspect of writing. And most of us who've enjoyed some success have been approached by someone with a brilliant idea (as judged by them) that merely requires a little typing on our part to become a bestseller—with them obviously being credited as co-author and pocketing half of the royalties.

But there's some truth in the popular perception. If you're telling a conventional story, the development of a *premise*, possibly expressed in a single sentence, is the most critical phase of your project. In some form, it will go in the enquiry letter to an agent or publisher, on the cover of your book and on posters for the movie adaptation. Plenty of writers will tell you that it's not their best-written books but the ones with the compelling premises that have been most successful.

Even in literary and experimental fiction, the concept, though it may not be expressed in the same way as a more plot-oriented premise, is important. It's the book that you're writing, the project you're putting a substantial part of your life into, and you need to be clear on what it is.

And yet…when I run workshops for writers who have at least begun drafting their manuscript, many—most—of them struggle to explain what it's about and, particularly, the story that it's telling.

> *It's set in a dystopian world, post-apocalypse…*
>
> *It's about my grandmother, but fiction.*
>
> *It's about the oppression of [insert minority group].*
>
> Or even: *It's not a conventional novel.* (Fine, but what is it?)

This is not to downplay the importance of place, character, themes and innovation, and indeed they may be intrinsic to your concept. But if you're going to tell a story, and take a planned approach to it, you need to have at least a sense of the plot: what's going to happen in the place you've chosen or world you've created, what journeys your characters will take and what decisions they'll face, what events and conflicts will bring to life the issue you want to explore. If you're not telling a story, you're still doing something: be clear on what that is.

If you're planning a novel primarily to explore a character, the character may be all you have at this point. I suggest you ask: what situations would best test and showcase that character? And you'll have the beginnings of a character-driven story.

The Rosie series began with the character of Don Tillman, a

socially awkward man whom I saw as struggling to fit in and be accepted. What situation would best highlight that? I landed on the search for a partner, since, in contemporary Western society, it's a quest full of subtle social conventions in which there is no obligation to be 'accepting' of someone you don't want to pair with.

Your concept is so important that it's worth applying your best creative efforts to coming up with and refining it over an extended period, and not starting your writing project until you are comfortable with it. Debut novelists frequently say that the idea had been brewing in their heads for a long time. And frequently those debuts are their most successful books. I suspect there's a connection. So, always have some ideas brewing and let them brew a while.

Practically, that means being on the lookout for concepts and allocating some of your creative time to thinking about them. It doesn't have to be every day, but about once a month I devote a little time to thinking about what I'll be working on next...and beyond that.

Creatively this is the toughest phase, because there are almost no restrictions. Once you have a concept, you'll be working more or less within its boundaries. But right now, for the only time in the project, it's wide open.

If you're waiting for inspiration, I suggest you use the time to write a short story or essay or poem or otherwise work on your writing. Don't waste your novel-writing energies on anything other than a concept you're happy with and excited about.

If you're writing a story of any kind, you should be aiming to produce a clear and concise summary of what it will be about—the premise—plus supporting notes. A good way to express your premise is in the form of a *logline*, like those you see in a TV or movie guide: a one- or two-sentence summary of the plot and its main challenge or conflict. The focus is on the set-up, rather than the complications or ending: if you have ideas for these, they can go in the supporting notes.

Loglines are an important marketing tool for screenwriters, so there's plenty of advice around on writing them. As a novelist, your primary concern is to clarify and express your thoughts for your own guidance. Look at a few loglines (IMDB is a good source) and you'll get the idea, along with evidence that they can be constructed even for the most unconventional works. Here are a few:

> *During WWII, a German businessman uses his resources to*
> *save Jews from the concentration camps. (*Schindler's List /
> Schindler's Ark*)*
>
> *When a video of Bart and Homer fighting goes viral, they become*
> *social-media celebrities. (An episode of* The Simpsons*)*
>
> *The lives of two mob hitmen, a boxer, a gangster's wife, and a*
> *pair of diner bandits intertwine in four tales of violence and*
> *redemption. (*Pulp Fiction*)*

And at the more experimental end of the scale:

> *A nurse is put in charge of a mute actress and finds that their*
> *personae are melding together. (*Persona*)*
>
> *A dying man in his forties remembers his past: his childhood, his*
> *mother, the war, personal moments and things that tell of the*
> *recent history of all the Russian nation. (*The Mirror*)*

Putting your premise in this form is the endgame of this stage. Along the way, your expressions of it are likely to be messy, half-formed and contradictory, as you kick around possibilities on paper and in your head.

But where *do* we get our ideas in the first place? And how do we ensure they're original?

Writing what you know

I'll start with some tough love. There's a compound word that sets off alarm bells for me—memories of too many writers who've spent years with a project that they seem unable to bring to fruition, who labour mightily for little output and much angst, and, even if they manage to finish the manuscript, find that it's disjointed, uninteresting and self-indulgent.

That word is *semi-autobiographical*. If it applies to the novel you're contemplating, I'd counsel you to rethink. That goes double if it's your first novel, when you'll have the added load of learning process and craft. It's such a common problem—I'd say it's second only to pantsing as a reason that authors get stuck—that I'll spend a few paragraphs explaining and arguing.

But wait. What about *write what you know*? Surely we know ourselves better than we know anyone. Really? Think about your friends. How honest are they with themselves about their strengths, weaknesses and motivations—attributes that others may see in flashing lights? Ah, you say, but writing will be a journey of personal discovery...therapy, if you like.

That's a road not to be taken lightly. Serious therapy is a long, demanding and often painful process. Perhaps—*perhaps*—writing a book is a substitute for working with a professional therapist, or indeed, working alone on your self-knowledge. If you want to find out, that's your choice. But my experience tells me that if your writing carries the burden of coming to terms with your past, your wounds, your demons, it will take so much of your energy that you'll have little left for good storytelling. Of course, if you're pursuing personal insight or peace of mind rather than the best novel you can write, that's a different matter. Just be sure to acknowledge that goal and understand you will likely face an even tougher road and less chance of publication than more detached novelists.

What about memoir—surely that's even harder than *semi-*autobiographical writing? Apparently not: writers routinely manage to write memoirs without tying themselves in knots—at least not inextricably—and I'm confident that this book can help them. I'm not saying it's easy, particularly when you dig below the surface of events to look at motivations and impact, as you should.

While I was working on *The Rosie Result*, I was asked to write a personal essay for a collection and thought there would be synergy in writing about my own childhood, which had some parallels with Hudson's. That six-thousand-word essay took more out of me than the entire novel did.[5] I'm sure it helped the novel, and probably my own self-awareness, but it's not a piece I'm proud of in a literary sense. And it was only an essay, not a book.

But two factors give the memoir writer an advantage over the semi-autobiographical novelist. The first lies in that elimination of *semi*. The commitment to truth removes one big choice from the writing—what to be honest about and what to make up. In my experience, these decisions are more about what the author is prepared to share than what will contribute to a satisfying story for the reader. Such decisions can be confronting and stressful—and distracting.

Second, the reader does not expect the same adherence to story

---

[5]   The essay, 'Rewiring', appears in the 2019 anthology *Split: True Stories of Leaving, Loss and New Beginnings*, edited by Lee Kofman.

structure from the memoir writer as from the novelist. Knowing the author is constrained by the facts, they will cut them some slack in dramatic rhythms, convenient coincidences and dangling threads. Fidelity kills invention, and the reader may allow for that *if they know it's a true story*.

The bottom line: I recommend you write a memoir *or* make up a story. Beware of letting your novel fall between the two stools.

So how do you *write what you know*? You do it by using your deep knowledge of some place, profession or culture—or, indeed, personal situation—that readers may be unfamiliar with to tell a story, but not your own story.

My character Don Tillman drew on my knowledge of 'geeks'— including myself—acquired through a life in science and information technology, plus ham radio, wine collecting, and my share of awkward dates. But his life was not my life. Not even in a *semi* sense. I invented a story; my experience informed it.

That's one starting point: a field, a domain, that you know about. It's not the only way.

A writer I know was listening to two elderly men—a longstanding couple—discussing in a radio interview the challenges of having to admit one of them to a nursing home that was aligned with his religion but not so comfortable with his sexual orientation. The writer was young, not particularly connected to the gay male community, with little knowledge of dementia and the religion in question. But she was profoundly moved by the story. As she imagined a novel about these men, she created a nationality and job history for one of them, again outside her direct experience. But she devoted time—a lot of time—to research and the novel is now well advanced.

Passion may also drive to you to a social, ethical or political topic on which you hold a strong position. At the time I began writing

The Rosie Project, I had a view of Asperger's syndrome (as it was then called) as a difference rather than a deficit—basically, 'Guys like Don are fine and an important part of a diverse world'—though I'd never really articulated it. It wasn't something I was particularly passionate about, though I think my position ultimately came through fairly clearly.

By the time I got to *The Rosie Result*, ten years later, I was better informed: I'd discussed my first novel with autism experts, attended conferences and was in touch with people in that community, including many activists. And my position was clear: I was firmly in the neurodiversity (as distinct from the 'disease / deficit') camp.

Paradoxically, this time it was harder to write a novel—or at least a good novel—that incorporated that view. Because if you set out to send a message, you'll likely do it so unsubtly that you'll alienate your readers, even those who agree with you. People don't pick up a novel looking to be harangued.

If you hold a strong position, I suggest you choose a story that's in your area of concern, then tell it as honestly as you can. Don't turn your hero into your mouthpiece—a 'self-insertion' or 'Mary Sue'. Your views will permeate the story anyway, but less intrusively. (As a pre-teen, I consumed Robert Heinlein's science-fiction novels, and even at that age began to mentally push back against his stock older-male-mentor character with his predictable set of political views.)

More broadly, most authors will tell you that themes are emergent rather than deliberately placed. There's no need to nominate them now. If you do, you may find them subsumed by others as you write. And that's generally a good thing.

I'm inspired by real-life events and people, particularly those I'm close to. Being close means that I can observe or recall small details. But the word is 'inspired': I feel no obligation to render them faithfully or to include *all* the details. A friend of mine did undertake something like Don's wife project that kicks off *The Rosie Project*, but the similarity ends there. The key words are *what if? What if* something more exciting, more interesting, more story-like, had happened?

There was a time I agreed to Anne inviting an old flame of hers to join us at our holiday home for a few days. It all went fine—no drama, so no story—but I asked myself *what if? What if* the flame had reignited? And that was the seed that grew into *The Best of Adam Sharp*. But, as I'm quick to assure people who think I must have personally experienced every moment in that story, it was just a seed.

The quest for originality

No matter what your concept, someone will tell you it's been done before. If it's relatively simple, they're probably right to some degree: *Two mismatched cops set out to solve a murder; our protagonist, suffering memory loss, tries to piece together their past; a young woman and a handsome widowed doctor fall in love.*

Stories of solving crimes and falling in love have been told innumerable times, but readers still buy the books. If you're not (consciously or unconsciously) copying something already out there, it's likely that your story details, characters and writing style will be different enough that you won't be sued—and that readers who may have already read something similar will still be interested.

For much the same reasons, I wouldn't worry too much about your idea being stolen. I see it in writing classes: students not prepared to disclose anything about their project in case it gets ripped off. Plagiarism of this kind seems to be rare. Perhaps, sadly, your idea isn't all that interesting to other writers.

However, I would counsel you *not* to take the next step of reading or watching whatever book, movie, play or TV series your friends are recommending as being 'just like what you're doing'. *The Big Bang Theory* premiered a few months after I started work on *The Rosie Project*. (The short story that introduced Don Tillman had already been published, so I can claim precedence!) and everyone was telling me I needed to see it. The parallels were obvious: in my early drafts, Don was a physicist (I'd studied physics, so was writing what I knew).

I resisted the temptation and was glad I did. If you're working similar territory, you're going to find similar material. That's natural, but if I'd seen it in someone else's book or TV show I'd have felt conflicted: did I come up with this independently or did I steal it? How could I prove it?

Also, I'd be discouraged, intimidated. I'd be looking at work in the same space as mine that was fully refined. If I'd seen it while I was writing a draft, I might well have felt I couldn't do any better and abandoned the project. As I wrote the Rosie series, I never watched *The Big Bang Theory* or read Mark Haddon's *The Curious Incident of the Dog in the Night-Time*, the reference points for writing about 'Asperger's syndrome'.

But, originality.

One option is the 'high concept'—the idea so wild that nobody else is likely to have thought of it. A man remains the same age as his portrait grows old. A web-footed woman tries to retrieve her heart after her husband loses it gambling. *As Gregor Samsa awoke one morning from uneasy dreams, he found himself transformed in his bed into an enormous insect*. The nature of these concepts is such that they tend to take you into the world of science-fiction, fantasy or the surreal, which is fine if that's where you want to go. I've never had a concept as high as these that I felt like developing further and can't offer you any reliable process for finding one.

My approach to finding original concepts uses the 'experiment with combinations' technique that I mentioned Chapter 3, on creativity—in this context, a *mash-up*. It's exemplified by the common plot formulation of 'x meets y': '*Pride and Prejudice* meets *Dracula*.'

As recommended in Chapter 2, I keep a list of ideas: for stories, characters, places, structures, writing modes—any of the elements of a novel or short story. I include things I know and topics I'm fascinated by or passionate about. When I'm ready to start thinking about my next project, well in advance of formally kicking it off, I choose the item that appeals most, then look for synergies with others on the list.

The Rosie Project pulled together two ideas: an autistic man searching for the ideal partner (inspired, as noted above, by real life), plus a concept I'd suggested to Anne some years earlier and that she'd abandoned: a woman searching for her biological father via surreptitious DNA testing. I'd already made progress with the first idea; to add the second, I had to make Don a geneticist instead of a physicist, but my pay-off was that I now had two characters trying to find happiness through an idealised other.

When a socially challenged genetics professor sets out to find the perfect partner, he meets a totally unsuitable woman who enlists him in a quest of her own.

Some years back, I thought of writing about a marathon that put me in hospital—a true story. By itself, not so interesting. Pheidippides famously *died* running the first one. But as I scanned my ideas list, I spotted an entry that had come from an early writing class where we'd discussed choice of tense (past, present, future) and point of view (first, second, third person). I'd thought it would be interesting to write a story that employed all six modes. And to signal my intent, I'd start with the least conventional combination: second-person future. *You will.* That's what you say to yourself at the beginning of a marathon, and what the marathon champion who revved us up before we started had said: *You will need to dig deep.* There was the synergy I was seeking. I decided to write about my marathon using three combinations of person and tense. Storytelling techniques like this, while differentiating the final story, won't always make it explicitly into the logline.

When a middle-aged man tries to add a marathon to his bucket list, he gets a harsh reminder of his mortality and learns to better appreciate the present.

The resulting short story benefited from the changes of tone that the different combinations offered: the third-person–past-tense detachment I'd felt in the intensive-care unit and the first-person–present-tense immediacy of emerging back into the world.[6]

By the time I'd finished, the strict breaks in tense between sections had become mixed with other tense changes, though the story retained a sense of unusual usage. The shifts in person (first, second and third) remained. That's the way it works: the concept is there to provide inspiration—a starting point—and you refine as you proceed.

I've mentioned that *The Best of Adam Sharp* was a *what if?* about two former lovers meeting again. But I welded onto that another idea: a book with a 'soundtrack' achieved through references to popular songs, which I hoped the reader would hear in their head. I'm reasonably confident that while there are plenty of stories out there about rekindled love, and many stories that feature the songs

---

[6] You can read the final story at smh.com.au/entertainment/books/three-encounters-with-the-physical-20130111-2cl32.html

of the sixties and seventies, there aren't many that do both. Again, the extra dimension doesn't make it into the logline.

When a musician in a tired marriage is contacted by his ex-lover, he is pulled into her marital games and faced with a choice between comfortable companionship and the love of his life.

One more: I was thinking of structuring a story around the Beatles' iconic 'White Album', with each chapter inspired by one of the thirty songs. *Maybe* that hadn't been done before. But I still needed a story, and on my list I found an idea about a couple who wrote together (as Anne and I do). Some parallels with the Lennon–McCartney collaboration, perhaps. That became the starting point for my novella *Creative Differences*.

When a writing couple decide to pursue separate creative goals, they find themselves having to choose between their marriage and their careers.

The above premises all begin with 'When'. It's not obligatory, but it's a good formula: it gives us the inciting incident, and a sense of where the action is going and what the conflicts or challenges will be. The second clause is likely to become a turning point as we flesh out the story. And a big decision is always a good thing.

Biography and memoir

What about biography (including autobiography) and memoir? I've already flagged the downside of memoir and autobiography—the need for sometimes painful self-reflection and analysis. And openness: it's difficult to write a personal story that withholds information, and it's the most private and intimate information that the reader is keenest to know. If you want your book to be about your journey through psychotherapy, but not the problems you were dealing with, or your cycle trip around the world, but not the romantic encounters, you'll be writing with one hand tied behind your back.

The upside is that once you've decided to write a biography, presumably on the basis of knowing something about the subject, you pretty much have your concept. But, as with memoir (a collection of memories rather than a 'complete' life story), there's still a question of selection or angle. What to omit, what to emphasise? What story, of the many stories in a person's life, do you want to tell? When I wrote my marathon story—in itself, just a small part of my life—I did not mention that my admission to hospital was on my daughter's eighteenth birthday. I was conscious that if things didn't go well we might not see each other again, and that I was grateful for the recent hours I'd spent teaching her to drive. Those scenes and reflections would have made a story in themselves, but it wasn't the one I chose to tell.

A surgeon friend of mine who has undertaken important research and pioneered the participation of women in her specialty, as well as doing day-to-day clinical work, wanted to write a memoir and was faced with having to decide what aspect to focus on. And how much of her personal life—the sacrifices and personal challenges—to include. Her inclination was to emphasise the research. It was the most interesting aspect to her, but I felt she'd be missing some of the material of most appeal to the reader. She settled on keeping it open—deferring the cull until she'd come up with a first cut of the cards. (Another advantage of doing an outline first: she reduced the risk of throwing away tens of thousands of words.)

In contemplating a book about a business owner who'd taken an unconventional path to success, I had the option of examining his personal background (where did his approach come from?) or focusing on his business life. One book would be a psychological study, at least in part; the other would be more of an inspirational business book.

So, while you don't have to decide at this point, if you *can* narrow your focus, you'll avoid work on material that ultimately won't be included. And your synopsis can be very short, just identifying subject and scope: *A Biography of Auntie May—Spy* or *Dr O's Most Challenging Cases* or *How Kim Khan Wrote Her Own Rules for Business Success* are fine at this concept stage.

Reviewing your concept

As you work on your concept, make notes. You'll be mulling over characters, events and locations over an extended period. Get those ideas down so you don't lose them. After this, you'll be writing the synopsis (which we'll cover in the next two chapters). For that, you'll need to know the main characters, key turning points and dramatic question(s)—as described in Chapter 4—and the ending. You'll inevitably be thinking about at least some of those now.

Is the concept big enough?

There's a question you should ask at this stage and again when you've written the synopsis: is the concept big enough for a novel? Can it generate enough story? Will the journey we're about to send our characters on be long enough and complex enough to keep our readers engaged for the length of a novel?

The answer is usually yes, but if you can show me the first- and second-act turning points, I'll feel even more confident.

Conversely, you may have more than one story—which is hardly a bad thing. It's fine for one aspect of the story to end and another to begin: that's a turning point. Maybe the dramatic question will be replaced by another. But if the turning point feels like the climax—the high point emotionally in the story—you should consider making it the climax. That may mean discarding the rest or telling it out of sequence.

In an early version of *The Rosie Project* (at that stage *The Klara Project*), Don and Klara came together as a couple at the first-act turning point. This was workable, as the love story was there to set up the main narrative of their domestic life (and a brain tumour). Recovery from the brain tumour was the climax. But when I decided to focus on the love story, the conclusion of that became the climax, and the brain-tumour story was put on hold—permanently, as it turned out. Sometimes less is more.

Can you do the research?

Now is also the time to deal with any factors that might cause you to regret your choice after you've put in time and effort. Can you do any necessary research? If you're writing memoir or autobiography, are you prepared to answer the personal questions that the reader will have? In the case of non-fiction or fiction with a basis in real events, are there legal issues you need to consider before you invest time?

Appropriation—can you tell this story?

Appropriation—sometimes framed as 'stealing others' stories'—and representation of minorities is a hot topic among publishers and academics. It's easy to take a simplistic position, and many non-writers do. But if you want avoid doing inadvertent damage and alienating readers, including potential publishers, you'll do some research and familiarise yourself with the issues and arguments. As a bonus, you'll find that much of the advice on representing minority groups is good literary advice. Stereotyping, exoticisation and fridging (look it up!) are writing faults as well as ethically suspect. Our stories will be better and our characters more interesting if they portray—accurately and insightfully—the diversity of people and society.

I chose to write a trilogy with a first-person protagonist who is autistic—and I don't identify as autistic myself. The books have been well received, I think largely because the portrayal is sympathetic (people generally find Don decent and likeable) and based on real life, so I avoid some of the generalisations and negative framing of the textbook descriptions. I'm sure many in the autism community would rather they'd been written by an autistic person, but authenticity is no guarantee of publication (we can do something about that) or sales (tougher!). Sometimes people are happy to get positive representations out there any way they can.

If you're a member of a minority group, you may face different pressures: to advocate for that group, or at least to tell stories from that world.

Ultimately, you have to work out for yourself where you stand on this and other ethical issues. You need to do your research—we'll talk more about that in Chapter 8. And, if you take from individuals, a community or culture, you may want to think about what you are offering in return.

What's special about your concept?

Before you commit to your concept, you should ask: what's special about it? What is its biggest 'point of difference'? Character? Plot? Voice? Place? Any of these can take centre stage: in the Rosie books, it's Don's character and voice; in *The Best of Adam Sharp*, I was relying largely on plot; *Two Steps Forward* and *Two Steps Onward* were about place—the Camino de Santiago and the Chemin d'Assise / Via Francigena in France, Spain and Italy.

Will it be enough to make your novel stand out? Do you believe in it? If the answer is no, then it's back to the drawing board, or at least the daily creative routine. Ultimately, it's better to abandon an unpromising concept than to invest a substantial part of your life in it.

Case study

We'll finish with a look at our case study. The idea for *The Rosie Result* came from readers who told me that they'd love a book about Don Tillman's childhood. Autism is something that's strongly associated in the public mind with children, and autistic kids face specific challenges, notably coping with the structure and social environment of schooling. I wanted to do it, but the timeframe of the two existing novels put Don's schooldays in the 1970s, when knowledge of and attitudes to autism were different. I thought it would be more useful and engaging to explore current attitudes.

I came up with the idea that we could look at an autistic childhood in the present day through Don and Rosie's son, Hudson, serendipitously created in *The Rosie Effect*. Autism runs in families, so the premise was realistic.

I'd previously toyed with writing a conventional sequel to the first two books to explore Don's journey to self-awareness, in particular his own autism. I didn't consider combining the ideas until I got deep into the synopsis and saw the synergy: as Don (our narrator) tried to help Hudson, he would naturally reflect on his own childhood and possible autism. So ultimately—though not at the concept stage—the book was the combination of two ideas.

Even in its simpler version, the concept needed work: in particular, it lacked an inciting incident to raise a dramatic question and set Don and Hudson off on their journeys. I let the problem brew for a full year while I worked on another book. Eventually, I settled on Hudson's school asking for an autism assessment and Don deciding to share his knowledge of how to cope in an autism-unfriendly world.

When Don and Rosie are advised to have their son Hudson tested for autism, Don quits his job to coach him on fitting in.

Once I had that, I felt I'd done the most critical part of the task. The concept was strong enough to build on (and with the eventual addition of Don's own journey, would become stronger). The rest I knew how to do.

6
Synopsis—Plot

At the end of this stage, you'll have:

1. A draft synopsis (including title) focusing on plot
2. Supporting notes.

Nobody, it seems, likes synopses. An editor who spoke to our writing class said, 'We ask for a synopsis, but personally I don't read them, so don't sweat it.' (I did sweat it, and she was ultimately the editor who acquired *The Rosie Project*.)

Authors often see synopses the same way, as an annoying and extraneous addition to the submission package. Many struggle to write them, because (I would argue) the premise and structure of the story is not clear in their minds. And this is *after* they've completed their manuscript.

The foundations of your story should be as clear as you can make them, even before you start brainstorming plot ideas. So you need to write a synopsis now. It's not easy, but it doesn't have to be perfect—yet. What we're looking for is the inciting incident, the dramatic question(s), the key turning points and the ending. Plus the main characters, with the protagonist identified. Not much at all. But if you start writing without these foundations, you'll be pantsing.

This is not the synopsis you'll be sending to your agent or publisher. It's a document that you'll update as you proceed with the project and rewrite at the end. Because of that, you have no obligation to squeeze it into some word limit. On the contrary, throw everything about the story that you can think of into this version. The only reader is you—don't worry about pretty writing or explaining things you know. I usually end up with one or two pages.

We'll tackle the synopsis in two stages, in order to do justice to two crucial aspects: plot and character. Approaching it from these different perspectives will also encourage creative thinking.

In this chapter, we focus on plot, then, in the next, switch to character. It's not a clean split. You can't describe plot without mentioning who the characters are, at least to the extent of describing what they do to progress the story. And the actions that a character takes are what defines them for the reader. If you feel your story is more about character than plot, or that your ideas for character are clearer at this point, feel free to jump ahead and tackle that first.

Sometimes you've done enough thinking about the concept that this stage goes pretty easily. You probably have the inciting incident and the major characters—at least the protagonist(s)—in your mind. You may have the ending: if it's a romance, chances are the couple get together; if there's a crime, the story is likely to end with it being solved. The challenge is usually the turning points. Unless you've made a decision otherwise, I suggest you start with a three-act structure, which means you're looking at a minimum of three turning points—at the end of the first and second acts, plus the inciting incident. You're not locking yourself into three acts, but you are forcing yourself to make the action rise and fall at least three times.

If you have in mind something other than a three-act structure, you may not need these specific turning points or indeed the inciting incident, ending, characters or any turning points at all. Perhaps you're envisaging a series of vignettes or a long, meditative monologue with no twists and turns or a five-act structure in the manner of Shakespeare or network television. But you're envisaging *something*, or you don't have a project. You need to get that something down in as much detail as you can.

Trying it out

At any point prior to the drafting, you may like to write a chapter or two to try out your narrative voice and perhaps the voices of your main characters. You can do it once you have a part of the story—typically but not always the opening—clear in your mind. Or you can go earlier and try pantsing. You may keep some or all of the writing. Regardless, it will give you confidence that your planning is leading to something that you have the ability to translate into prose.

Tips on writing a draft synopsis

Here are a few tips to help you get there.

1. You've probably got a title in mind—a working title, at least. If you haven't, it's time to come up with one, and to put it down for regular creative attention until the book is locked into a publication schedule and the title is out there in the world. Add any alternative titles to the synopsis. Titles matter—a lot—and your publisher may offer their own suggestions, but you want to bring a great idea or two to

the table rather than rely on others. Plus, it's another way of focusing your creative mind on what the story's about.

2. The premise should give you guidance as to the dramatic question, the main challenge or conflict; the lowest point (second-act turning point), where the declared mission has failed; and the climax, where the dramatic question is resolved and our protagonist(s) may demonstrate growth by doing different from what they would have done at the beginning of the story. Expand and clarify.

3. As you think about the key plot points—and any others you've identified at this stage—think about the associated *decisions*. These are what drive the story. As we'll see in the next chapter, they are also our most important vehicle for showing character. Make clear not only the outcome of each decision but the choice faced and the implications: *Angelina wants Adam to stay in Australia to pursue their relationship, but Adam chooses to honour his international consulting contract, putting their future in jeopardy. Don decides to change himself in order to win over Rosie, at the risk of his own integrity. Zoe must choose between her lover and her best friend.* A couple of decisions like these can go a long way to defining your story.

4. Try working backwards from the ending / climax / final decision: think about how you see the story ending, then look at what will need to happen to set that up. As Stephen Covey's second habit of highly effective people says, *begin with the end in mind.* If we start with *Adam has to choose between his long-term partner and the love of his life*, we don't even need to know what that final decision will be. But we do know what we have to set up and we already have three characters.

5. Ask *whose story is this?* The thinking you've done so far will
    probably have given you a protagonist or protagonists, but if
    not, it's time to identify who (possibly more than one person)
    is making the decisions that drive the story forward. That's
    your protagonist, be they hero, antihero or villain. The story
    won't necessarily be told from their point of view—but it
    probably will. In *The Rosie Result*, there's a shift at the end
    of the second act (at the second-act turning point), where
    Hudson begins to drive the action, although Don continues
    to tell the story. That's an unusual move, but I was doing it to
    show Hudson's transition to personal autonomy. If I hadn't
    already established Don as the sole narrator through two
    earlier books, I might well have switched to Hudson's point
    of view.

6. It's normal to have more ideas for the set-up (first act) than
    for the later parts of the story. But you do want to know
    what drives the bulk of the story—the complications and
    escalation. At some point we have to get over the problem
    that many authors face of having a packed first act and not
    enough to put in the second. Best to start now.

7. If it's biography or memoir, you need to identify the main life
    events you intend to write about.

8. Note any subplots you're considering, but your focus at
    this stage should be on the main story—especially that final
    three-quarters. Beware of inserting subplots to make up for a
    lack of main story ideas.

Here is my synopsis for *The Rosie Result* (with earlier title) prior to
proceeding to the next stage. It took three drafts and about a month.

Feel free to skim it: I just wanted you to see a real one, warts and all, and to note my subsequent comments.

THE HUDSON PROJECT

Setting: Melbourne. Hudson is 10–11 (probably include 11th birthday), coming into final year of primary school.

Set-up: Hudson is completing primary school. He is autistic (similar to Don), and Don and Rosie want him to go to the associated (private) high school, which is tolerant etc., and not be held back. Don quits his job to take on the role of coach.

Dramatic Question: Will Hudson get accepted to the high school? (Resolution: Hudson makes his own choice to go to the 'special school' or a regular public high school.)

Major subplot: Don's career choices as he quits his job, establishes a bar, reviews his path forward, perhaps takes a job in private sector.

Secondary subplot: Rosie's career challenges as she returns to full-time (and demanding) research work.

Themes:

Group vs individual identity (esp. identifying as autistic)—incl. identity politics

How we bring up kids

Fitting in / acceptance

Inciting Incident: Hudson's school tells Don and Rosie that Hudson's not going to be ready for high school.

First Act Turning Point: Don quits his job to coach Hudson.

Second Act TP: Hudson screws up majorly, and now Don and
  Rosie have to fight the system.

Climax: Hudson makes his own call (but enabled to by his growth
  with Don and Rosie).

Key Characters: Don, Hudson, Rosie. Teacher / principal?

Other Ideas:

Things Don misses about NYC—alone in bars making conver-
  sation...social practice...perhaps there's a move toward
  Gene-ness as he acquires social confidence.

Phil—perhaps remarried now that Rosie's OK. Or include his
  new relationship.

Don's family?

George? Back to UK—didn't fit in...Or dead?

Pre-flight check in the car—less safe than plane.

Stopping coughing with handkerchief stuffed in mouth (on plane).

What about Sonia and Rosina?

At first glance, it may seem that I had it all worked out at this point.
But you don't have to look too closely to see that it's missing some
crucial plot details, particularly in the later parts of the story. What
does Hudson do to get into trouble? *Screws up majorly* does little
more than restate the generic second-act turning point ('all is lost' /
'the hero hits their lowest point') in the context of this particular
dramatic question. We don't know how he screws up or how he
gets out of it.

Plus there's the whole second act—half the story, if we follow
the guidelines on proportions—described only by Don's intent to
'coach him on fitting in'. Five words for half the book. If I was

reviewing someone else's synopsis, I wouldn't let them get away with that. And the 'other ideas' were no more than what the heading suggests—thoughts without much context. Besides answering the question *What about Sonia and Rosina?* none of them made it into the final plan, let alone the eventual novel. The two scene ideas are pretty terrible.

Fortunately, we're not finished with the synopsis. We'll now look more deeply at the characters who will drive and be illuminated by the plot we've outlined. That work will, in turn, stimulate further ideas for the plot.

7
Synopsis—Characters and Character

At the end of this stage, you'll have:

1. An improved synopsis
2. Profiles for the main characters.

I've occasionally bragged that I could write a passable episode of *The Simpsons*, or indeed almost any sitcom or serial drama you care to name. Many of my screenwriter friends would make the same claim. But what we're *not* saying is that we could create the series—the situation and, crucially, the characters. That's where the genius lies.

Turn this around. If you can create the right characters, people whose strengths, weaknesses and values will be showcased by the situation your premise places them in, story will come. As Harper Lee said, 'Characters make their own plot. The dimensions of the characters determine the action of the novel.' Great characters are the foundation of great stories. For most readers, they're also the access point to those stories.

The work you put into developing interesting characters will be paid off many times over in better story and easier writing. (And for anyone protesting that I've covered plot before characters, you'll see that this chapter is much longer.)

The core of my Rosie series was Don Tillman, and I knew that he would not only add his quirky, comedic perspective to whatever scene I put him in, but also suggest additional story simply by my asking, 'What will Don do in this situation?' Add even a peripheral antagonist like 'Rabbit' Warren, the sports teacher, or 'Judas' Lefebvre, Rosie's misogynistic boss, and the scenes almost write themselves.

We want our main characters, those who drive the story, to have the complexity and depth that will allow the decisions they make—and thus the turning points of the story—to be surprising and believable at the same time.

In developing our characters' personalities, their journeys, and how they change (their *arcs*), we not only lay the foundations for our descriptions of them (*telling* the reader) but generate ideas for actions that will *show* their attributes through the way they behave and respond to circumstances.

Drawing on real life

Where do our characters come from? As with plot, real life with a dose of *what if?* is a great source. People are people, whether they're living in the sixteenth century or in space: chances are, you know someone who embodies at least some of the attributes you're looking for in a character. I say 'some': it's been said that a fictional character is a third someone you know, a third yourself and a third made up.

I'd change 'someone you know' to 'several people you know' and raise that component to a half. And add: 'some of which you know about and some of which you include unawares / subconsciously'.

That qualification applies particularly to the component that comes from you; you're going to include aspects of yourself without or despite your efforts, so just let it happen. For the reasons I discussed in Chapter 5, I counsel against intentionally making a version of yourself a major character in the story.

You can be deliberate in the search, listing the key attributes of your characters and looking for them in others. I do this mentally—it's not the sort of thing you should leave evidence of. My character Adam Sharp is a piano-playing IT specialist from Manchester with commitment issues. Those four attributes were inspired and informed by separate people—in some cases more than one—and the musical reference in the name (A Sharp) was borrowed from a colleague. After all that, a psychiatrist friend read the draft and concluded that Adam was me.

Try *really hard* not to copy other fictional creations. Writers are great readers and screenwriters are great watchers of movies. Too often it shows in stereotypes who may have passed down several generations. Find and get to know a real boss or detective or priest—or several—in all their complexity and contradictions. Your knowledge of them can inform a character who feels real and fresh. You don't need to reprise Michael Corleone or Miss Marple or Father Ralph de Bricassart.

The advice to get to know real people is particularly pertinent when you're representing someone from a marginalised group. Generalisation is the enemy of vivid writing. People with mental illness are a good example. There are books on virtually every condition and guidelines on writing sensitively—but if that's all if you draw upon, your characters will be stereotypical and bland. Meet some, or, if you can't do that, read some memoirs (preferably) and biographies of real people with the relevant condition.

Watch for handed-down assumptions about age in particular. Grandmothers are not all little old ladies in shawls lost in their knitting. And if you're sixty, no matter how young you feel, the thirty-year-old character you're writing is different from you.

If you're looking for originality (as you should be), remember the trick with concepts: the conjunction of two otherwise unrelated ideas is a great way of generating something unusual. So, take two or more people or defining attributes, real or imaginary, and combine. In *The Rosie Result*, Gary is a violent homeopath—an unexpected combination, but by no means impossible or unbelievable, especially after he's been given an explanatory backstory.

Focusing on decisions

Let's take a closer look at our characters with a view to developing profiles for the main ones and revising our synopsis to clarify their roles. I suggest setting up a character-profiles document with a heading for each character.

You'll find dozens of tools for novelists and screenwriters that are supposed to help define your characters. Typically, they're in the form of questionnaires that cover everything from Myers-Briggs personality type to favourite TV show.

I don't use them: there are so many facets to a person, and we can only show a few of them in the limited space of a novel. There are real people I've known for years whose star sign and preferred drink I wouldn't be able to tell you. If a character needs to order a drink in the story, I'll choose one on the spot, consistent with other aspects of their background, and review it later. *But only if they order a drink*.

The superficial questions are supposed to prompt deeper exploration: *why* is Angelina's favourite drink a martini? But there's a better place to start digging: the decisions they make (or, if you don't have any story yet, the sorts of decisions they made in the past or *might* make in the story).

Nothing reveals character like decisions, be they considered or impulsive: we can *tell* the reader that Don does not bear grudges, but we'll *show* it to them when we give him the power to stop the person who got him fired from getting their own dream job. The twenty-three-year-old Angelina orders a fallen angel when she's trying to draw attention to herself and a martini when she's trying to appear sophisticated. At forty-five, she's worked out what she actually likes: a margarita. Some thinking went into those cocktail choices, but it was in the service of the story, not a separate character profile.

Conversely, if you're starting with character rather than plot (and even if you're just reviewing plot at this point), decisions can be your path to generating compelling story. As a starting point, ask yourself what two things your character wants most. Now create a situation that makes them choose between them. You may have defined your story's climax: Hudson must choose between pleasing others and being true to himself; Adam must choose between a comfortable life and a romantic dream; Zoe must choose between her lover and her lifetime soulmate.

We can then look behind these decisions, major and minor, and explore why they were (or will be) made. Actors have a succinct way of expressing it: *What's my motivation?* Answering that question, in the deepest way we can, is the most powerful and relevant way of fleshing out our characters, because it focuses on what the character does *in the story*, where it matters. Your synopsis, as it stands, should include a few crucial decisions, so it's an ideal starting point.

I've developed a technique for digging into a character's motivation that I find useful even at this early stage, where it not only helps to clarify characters, but to generate additional story. You'll continue to use it as your story develops and you introduce new decisions.

I focus on the most important decisions—the ones that shape the direction of the story—and how the character making those decisions would explain them. I ask three questions (and I'll refer to this as the *three-questions technique* from here on):

1. What would they tell their friends? I recognise that they might not be completely open, even with friends. This explanation might appear on the page, perhaps in dialogue.

2. What would they say to their (hypothetical) totally trusted therapist, after deep reflection? Now we're expecting not only for them to be open, but to dig below the surface, to the deepest level of their self-knowledge. The answer to this may appear in the protagonist's reflections or be implied through clues given to the reader.

3. What would our hypothetical (and astute) therapist, based on their longstanding knowledge of their client, tell us? We're trying to access the character's subconscious: aspects of their motivation that might come from past trauma, from the expectations and behaviour of their parents, and from unexpressed desires. The answer may inspire us to include past events that the reader will connect to present actions.

That final question can be challenging. Am I expecting you to be an armchair psychologist? An unqualified Freudian analyst? Absolutely. Fortunately, nobody's wellbeing is in your hands, but if you want to create interesting characters, you should acknowledge the role of unconscious motivations. The reader will at least sense them, if not see them as clearly as you do.

These questions take you several steps forward from the one-word motivations that authors too often provide, particularly for critical decisions that may be hard to understand. That one word is too often a personality type or disorder: *psychopath*, *paranoid*, or the all-purpose *mentally ill* and *evil*.

You can write a story in which motivations are defined by such shallow shorthand—and there are plenty of books in the crime and thriller genres in which the bad guys seem to have little reason for their actions and life choices. If the plot is intriguing or thrilling enough, or there's enough depth in the protagonist's portrayal, readers may not care. But only cartoon characters get up in the morning, twirl their moustaches and set their minds on doing evil. If you take the trouble to give the 'evil' antagonist a properly considered goal, belief system or trauma that motivates their behaviour, your story will be richer for it.

At this stage you will only need to examine two or three decisions in depth—likely made by one or two characters. As you proceed, you may add a few more. You'll find that they establish a basis for more minor decisions (which you'll want to be consistent with the major ones) and will frequently suggest scenes or reflections that set up the necessary background. You're generating story that will pay off in important ways.

If you're writing memoir or biography, your mindset will be different, but I'd still recommend trying this exercise.

In *The Best of Adam Sharp*, the most difficult decision to motivate believably was not Adam's choosing to reconnect with Angelina, his former lover, but his leaving her in the first place. What sort of guy is going to walk away from the love of his life? Why? After a lot of thinking, the answers to my questions came out something like this:

1. He'd tell his *friends* that he was bound by his work contract, which required him to travel for the next year. If Angelina was keen enough, she'd wait for him.

2. He'd tell his *therapist* that Angelina wanted to have children, his father was a bad role model and he was afraid he'd be the same. He wasn't ready to commit and was using work as an excuse.

3. The *therapist* would tell us that Adam was afraid that he wasn't good enough for Angelina and that she would abandon him—so he's getting in first. Adam's fear is rooted in the belief (not uncommon in children of separated parents) that his father abandoned the family because Adam wasn't good enough to keep him there. It's a deep wound he doesn't want to risk reopening.

Before I answered question three, Adam didn't have much of a background besides coming from Manchester and playing piano. Now I could give him a father whom he worshipped (I made him a professional musician) but who had chosen to walk out. His father would always be his hero, which was going to annoy his long-suffering mother no end—and offer opportunities for a little comedy. Plenty of new, and relevant, material there.

When he explains to Angelina why he's leaving, he's as open as he can be—he tells her what he'd tell his trusted therapist. As I answered these questions, I wasn't just making stuff up, throwing in random qualities, but fleshing out an integrated, consistent person and his family of origin.

Then there was the question of why Angelina didn't wait for him or throw in her own job to travel with him. Another round of analysis and insights.

I do have a head start here: my wife and writing partner is a psychiatrist. If delving into the psyche is not your forte, you might pose your questions to a friendly therapist—or anyone fascinated by unconscious motivation. 'What sort of background would lead to someone becoming a philanderer? Or serial killer? Or being attracted to Don Tillman?' Chances are your friend will enjoy speculating and seeing their wisdom on the page and their name in the acknowledgments—and you'll have some food for thought.

In *The Rosie Result*, one decision is central to the story's direction: at the first-act turning point, Don quits his job to coach Hudson on fitting in. Crucially (or it wouldn't be a decision), he has a choice. Many parents would trust the school's advice to get their child assessed for autism. And they'd likely not have quit their job so hastily.

As I looked at Don's decision, I realised it was actually *three* decisions: to reject the school's advice, to quit his job and to coach Hudson. They're related, but they could be separated—to give us three strong story moments rather than one.

Let's start with the decision to ignore the school's recommendation. Don is an established character, who to date has shown respect—even naive respect—for professional advice in various contexts.

1. He would tell his *friends* that he knows Hudson better than the principal does, and that Hudson's problems at school are no worse than those that Don himself faced as a child. Don's experience in his twenties of being

incorrectly diagnosed and hospitalised has made him
wary of mental-health interventions.

2. He would tell his *therapist* that he was shaken by the
    suggestion of Hudson's autism. People have suggested
    that he could be autistic himself: it's a place he doesn't
    want to go.

3. The *therapist* would seize on Don's concern about being
    labelled autistic himself. Despite what Don professes to
    believe, he sees autism as a negative and is afraid that
    Rosie does too.

The decision to quit his job:

1. Don would tell his *friends* that he's merely bringing
    forward the inevitable. He's committed a serious
    faux pas and it's been suggested he offer autism as an
    explanation. He's not prepared to do that, for good
    ethical reasons.

2. Don would tell his *therapist* that he just wants to leave
    a place where people label him as autistic, and make a
    new start.

3. The *therapist* would say that Don, in walking away
    from the shelter of academe, is not only avoiding
    confronting his possible autism, but trying to build a
    case against it by proving he can make it in the wider
    world.

One more—the decision to coach Hudson:

1. Don would tell his *friends* that it's a natural thing for a father to do (Don's father tried to do the same for him) and that he has good experience in overcoming social awkwardness.

2. Don would tell his *therapist* that he's out to prove that Hudson isn't autistic.

3. The *therapist* would say that Don is projecting his own experiences as a child onto Hudson, repeating a family pattern. He's in danger of identifying too closely and becoming blind to Hudson's different needs.

That's quite a lot, and it's not perfect. But it unearthed at least one crucial idea: that the story is not only about Hudson's journey to acknowledge his autism, but also about Don's. Don is our protagonist: it makes sense that the climax of the story will be *Don's* acknowledgment that he's autistic, prompted by Hudson's. This was an important development of the original synopsis. And there's a mention of Don's experiences as a child. It suggested that I should include his childhood reflections in the story—and his family of origin as characters.

Doing that gave my story a different climax and a personal journey to take Don there. It seemed embarrassingly obvious when I realised that Don's journey could parallel Hudson's, and that his reflections on his childhood in an earlier time would add a counterpoint to his son's. The idea had doubtless been sitting in the back of my mind for a long time. But, as I have Don say in another context, 'As with so many breakthroughs, the answer was obvious in retrospect.' This was the point at which I became confident I had the foundations for a strong story.

Smaller decisions also show character: early in *The Rosie Result*,

Don gets a call from the school because Hudson has had a meltdown on an excursion to the snow. He unhesitatingly jumps in the car and heads for the mountains, missing an important disciplinary hearing at work. I'll spare you the three-question analysis, but we're showing his care for his son, his respect for Rosie's work commitments in not passing the buck to her and his ambivalence about his job.

At another point, Hudson sacrifices his chance to win a race in order to help his disabled friend. The noble decision changes the school's view that Hudson is autistic, but later we learn that Hudson did it deliberately to create that impression. Our understanding of Hudson shifts with our understanding of the motivation behind his decision.

We can use the three-questions technique not only on decisions that take place within the novel's timeline, but on critical decisions that the character took in the past. Why does Don devote time to martial-arts training? Why did Rosie enrol in a PhD? Why didn't Adam Sharp pursue his musical ambitions?

Character arcs

A universal element of storytelling is that the protagonist, and sometimes other characters, will undergo a transformation, either intrinsically and / or in terms of how we perceive them as the story unfolds. *Character arc* is fundamental to the Hero's Journey and adds depth to even a heavily plot-driven story, with the change—usually in the positive direction—creating an opportunity for a big emotional moment.

You can think of the transformation in terms of the character's goals changing, typically from something explicit and pragmatic (outer goal) to something more personal and substantial (inner goal). Alternatively, you can frame it as a journey from what the character wants (superficial) to what they need (substantial), or as the overcoming of a flaw.

I find the three-question technique useful here too. If we interrogate what a character wants, to see where that desire comes from, we may find the deeper need. Hudson (and Don) *want* to be accepted by others. But behind that is a lack of comfort with who they are. Their *need* is to accept themselves.

The strongest portrayal of change is a decision, key to the direction or resolution of the story, that the reader realises is different from the one that the character would have made earlier. Sometimes it's made explicit by the character facing essentially the same choice at two different points—'before' and 'after'.

In the last sentence of the final chapter of *The Rosie Result*, Don announces to his assembled friends and family that he's autistic and proud of it. This contrasts with his decision in the book's first act to leave his job rather than identify as autistic.

Chances are you've identified some decisions of this kind already, but there may be room to do more. Ask yourself if and how each of your major characters could change in the course of the story, and begin thinking about how you'll show those changes.

Making characters relatable

While we're focused on the major characters: Kurt Vonnegut said, 'Give the reader at least one character he or she can root for.' Many readers of popular fiction want to identify with someone they find 'likeable' (which is not necessarily the same as 'good' or 'worthy') and they'll want that person to be a significant player in the story, typically the protagonist. Read a few online reviews and you'll see how much those factors influence readers' take on a book. You may find that disappointing and shallow, but the reality is that many read for a form of escapism that involves walking in the shoes of someone they can relate to.

This can be challenging when our protagonist is, on the surface, a person whom readers might avoid in real life. My early readers of the (then) screenplay of *The Rosie Project* were concerned that audiences would find Don's unusual behaviour annoying and unrelatable. The risk was that they'd see him as 'other', which was antithetical to my goal of bringing them into his world.

There are a number of techniques we can use to make a character likeable and relatable, and I used most of them in *The Rosie Project*.

1. They can 'pat the dog' or (per the title of Blake Snyder's screenwriting book) 'save the cat'—do something decent and worthy, preferably within the context of the story rather than gratuitously tacked on. Don cares for an elderly woman, and she in turn earns her place in the story by suggesting he would make someone a wonderful partner.

2. We can give them skills and personal qualities that our readers will enjoy appropriating as they identify with the protagonist. Don's a martial-arts expert, vanquishing a couple of overreaching bouncers.

3. We can have them do things that readers would love to do themselves: Don has a ball making cocktails and takes down the medico who tries to make fun of him.

4. We can surround our character with less-likeable people—if our reader wants to relate to someone, they're left with no other good options. I introduced Don at the same time as his philandering friend Gene and a patronising autism worker, and delayed Rosie's entry until well into the story, so readers

could not choose to identify with her until Don had had a chance to make his case.

5. We can explain their behaviour by showing why they became bitter or antisocial or 'broke bad'. In a novel, unlike in a movie or TV show, we are (usually) able to describe our protagonist's inner world. Don gets a chance to outline the unfamiliar but logical rationale for his behaviour, and, as a first-person narrator, he's our guide. We're inclined to trust guides.

6. We can give them a challenging goal. Our story may (and should) already do that. The challenge may be physical, psychological and / or in the form of formidable antagonists. It may be relatable specifically—Don's looking for a life partner— or only in the broad sense that it's a goal of some kind. If the character pursues their goal with dedication, resourcefulness and courage, the reader will be inclined to support them.

7. We can throw trouble at them in the form of antagonists, misfortune and their own mistakes, to elicit the reader's sympathy. (Rosie's stepfather doesn't approve of Don; Don gets caught trying to obtain DNA to help Rosie find her biological father; and, in the tradition of romantic comedies, Rosie initially rejects his proposal.)

8. We can withhold unappealing information until the reader is committed to being on their side—common in crime and thrillers, but we need to be confident the reader will not bail out after perceiving a breach of trust. In *Gone Girl*, we learn of Nick's infidelity (infidelity being a big turn-off for some readers) only after we are well into the story. For some, the information that Don has spent time in a psychiatric hospital might bring to mind negative stereotypes.

With those tools in our armoury—especially the challenging goal—we should be able to get readers onside with protagonists who are not traditionally 'good' or likeable: the criminal whose expertise and resourcefulness draws the reader into their mission, the comedic character and their ludicrously ambitious goal, the physician who's too busy saving lives to be civil to others.

If not, we're going to have to rely on fascination, curiosity and / or a compelling plot. *Lolita*, *American Psycho* and *The Collector* prove it can be done, and done brilliantly and successfully.

I like to think *The Rosie Project* offers all of those things too. Don is an intriguing character: many readers report that he gave them some insight into autism. And we have strong dramatic questions: *Will Don find a partner / get together with Rosie?* and *Who is Rosie's biological father?*

Finally, we can abandon hope that the reader will identify with the protagonist and offer them an alternative: a secondary character who, while not being the driver of the story, is caught up in the events—perhaps the cop seeking to bring the criminal protagonist to justice.

What about multiple protagonists? Some novels shift the point of view among two or more characters. We may want to give the reader a taste of an antagonist's plans so we can build suspense as they play out without the hero's knowledge. Or we may want to show both sides of a love story, or perhaps all sides of a family drama.

If we keep switching the point of view, we'll make it harder for the reader to identify with any single person's journey but may be able to tell a more complex story by showing different perspectives and motivations.

Readers can become invested in a multiple-person situation. Most can relate to a couple or family or team and imagine ourselves as a member, dependent on the collective outcome. Or we can step back a little further and ask the reader to care about the outcome of people who (typically) share some collective challenge, be it climbing a mountain or helping each other overcome their psychological wounds. Mary Lawson's *A Town Called Solace* is a nice example of the latter, with three protagonists, a mix of first-person present tense and third-person past tense and, as a bonus, some interesting treatment of time.

More characters

With the motivation for the big decisions sorted, we can look beyond the protagonist(s) to the other major characters—typically between three and eight in total. In the synopsis, we've likely mentioned only a few: it's a good time to think about who else should be in the story. As part of this, you should think about two obvious roles: antagonists and allies.

The obstacles our heroes face are not always human—they may be physical or personal or institutional. Even then, it's worth seeing if it's possible to create an antagonist to personalise the challenge and conflict. In *The Rosie Result*, I wanted to have Don and Rosie fight 'the system'—broadly well-intentioned but rigid and possibly misinformed—over Hudson's autism assessment and prospects. I personalised it in the form of the school principal and Hudson's teacher. And as I worked on Rosie's arc, I thought it would be good to have someone making life difficult for her at work after she'd travelled to Australia to take up a new job. So, 'Rosie's boss' went on the list.

In movies, allies or 'buddies' not only lend assistance but allow our protagonists to voice their thoughts, since we can't see inside their heads. In a novel, we usually have access to at least one character's thoughts, but a buddy facilitates a 'show, don't tell' approach to communicating through dialogue. Unless we want to portray our hero as a loner (and perhaps even then), we want to show how they interact with people who are on their side.

In a sequel, we'll already have a cast of characters, and our readers will enjoy seeing them again. It's best to consider them as candidates for necessary roles rather than shoe-horning them in. Don's former co-researcher Simon 'Judas' Lefebvre fitted neatly into the role of Rosie's difficult boss, and his history with Don opened the door for him to talk to Don about Rosie. Keep them all in the profiles document as possible inclusions.

I'm not too formal about my character profiles: my main concern is getting down their big decisions, the motivation behind them, their arcs and any unusual characteristics, together with ideas for scenes, reflections and even dialogue. I'll add details like age, gender, cultural background, ethnicity, disposition and speech patterns where they seem important to the story or will add interest to the character. In some cases, you may already have established these: they may be part of a character's identity and may contribute to their behaviour in the story. Character profiles for the main characters may run to a page; for the secondary characters, just a paragraph or so.

Such external *characterisation* (as distinct from the deep *character* that manifests itself in decisions) is what writing questionnaires usually focus on. If you do want to use questionnaires or write biographies, now is the time, after you've got the motivation for the big decisions sorted.

I also review some of my lazy assumptions: as a straight, white, able, middle-aged male, I'm conscious that I'm inclined to make too many characters in my own image—and signal it with their names: Don, Gene and Simon. Everybody's gender, race, nationality, disabilities and sexual orientation are on the table when I'm writing (but note my comments on appropriation in Chapter 5).

Changing these will affect characters' likely backstories and the assumptions readers—and you—will make about them. It seldom stops them playing the role you'd planned, and makes them and the story more realistic and interesting.

In *The Rosie Result*, my characters, several of them central to the story, include Minh (Vietnamese); Amghad (Egyptian); Allannah (African-Asian); Beatrice (Ghanaian); Laszlo (Hungarian); Julie (Czech); David Borenstein and Isaac Esler (Jewish); Tazza (Greek, gay, autistic); Sonia (Italian heritage); Professor Lawrence (lesbian); Liz (lesbian, autistic); Carl, Trevor and Merlin (gay); Blanche (who has albinism); and numerous autistic men, women and children, notably our two main characters. I haven't had any feedback to suggest this representation was excessive or distracting: Melbourne is a diverse city.

In contrast to the analysis I've asked you to do for the main characters, I'd encourage you to leave the supporting cast loosely defined so that, at least to some extent, they can be moulded—on the fly—to fit the requirements of the story. We don't want them locked down so hard that we can't play with the dynamic between character and story.

Names

At some point you have to give names to your characters, though they can be changed right up to the final edit. Some writers agonise over this and I'm one of them. Often a name feels very right—or very wrong—for no strong reason. I suspect it's due to historical associations, and you need to remember that your readers won't make the same connections unless the names are associated with well-known real or fictional identities. But it helps me feel comfortable with my creations. Readers often don't remember characters' names, even protagonists'. But you don't want names that are confused or forgotten while the reader is still reading.

Dave the Baseball Fan was originally Dan the Baseball Fan but the producers of the *Rosie Project* screenplay felt it was too similar to Don. This problem is more likely to arise if the names are unfamiliar to readers (e.g. multiple Japanese names for an Anglophone audience). Gene's name was suggested by a friend at a very early stage, when I'd cast him as a physicist. It was only later that I made him a geneticist: unconscious creativity surely at work.

I like to use not-too-common names for characters who will appear just a few times in the story—but whom we want our readers to recall. And, without descending into caricature, I sometimes use names that the reader may connect with some attribute of the character. So, in *The Rosie Project*, the department head's personal assistant is Regina, a name that many will associate with *queen*. I thought of her as reigning over the department, as personal assistants sometimes do, and hoped readers might subconsciously make the same connection. Hudson's friend with albinism is unfortunately named Blanche, and there is, of course, a story to explain it. Nicknames allow us to make the connection with personal characteristics explicit: Rosie calls her boss Judas because she believes he's betrayed her.

Combining characters

Now that we know who our main characters are, can we combine any of them? Something I learned from screenwriting is that actors are looking for 'meaty' roles, so a few complex characters with plenty of screen time are more attractive than a host of smaller walk-ons. Viewers and readers, in turn, can find it hard to keep track of a large cast, *A Song of Ice and Fire* (*Game of Thrones*) notwithstanding. It's worth taking opportunities to reduce their numbers.

Don's unreliable but ultimately loyal friend Gene was originally two people: the kind and helpful laboratory manager, giving Don sound advice, and the original Gene, an unadulterated rogue. Two stereotypes that we've seen a thousand times. By combining them, I created a more interesting character, or at least a more complex one. Hudson's class teacher and the physical-education teacher were separate individuals; in primary school the roles are often combined, so I did this and gave the non-sporting kid no escape from his least favourite subject.

Case study

As I finished my character-based review of the synopsis for *The Rosie Result*, I had profiles for Don, Rosie and Hudson—the three main characters. Below are my rough notes on Hudson. They're messy, incorporating a few new plot ideas that arose as I continued to think about the story, but, at least in a sketchy way, I had a set-up (request for autism assessment), some sense of the story ('man-up' lessons), a low point (suspension from school, indicating failure) and a resolution (acceptance of autism).

There's just the one key decision and a simple analysis. But combined with the picture of Hudson that was growing in my head, this profile was enough to go forward with.

PROFILE—HUDSON

Hudson is 12, undiagnosed autistic, bright, articulate, but struggling socially.

Accepts Don's help in the hope of fitting in.

2nd Act turning point: Brings a knife to school to dissect a pigeon (school calls Don in, cruelty to animals, knife…suspended).

Rejects Don's help: will solve the problem himself.

Would tell friends: I'm OK, I can handle this.

Would tell therapist: Wanted to prove to my parents that I was OK.

Therapist would say: He's struggling between finding himself and being what he thinks his parents want him to be.

Resolution: Joins online autism group (after an online self-assessment) and finds his tribe.

Ideas:

Don reflects on inevitability of Hudson being a nerd—Rosie has some autism symptoms too.

Don relates how he previously taught Hudson various things—strange foods, pain, shoes?

Don argues with counsellor who wants Hudson assessed for 'Autism Spectrum Disorder'. Maybe refuses a diagnosis.

Hudson sent to Phil for 'man-up' lessons; Phil plays chess with him and explains to Don & Rosie.

Hudson has some issue at school with kid with albinism (parents are anti-science) and at some point resolves.

Hudson's birthday party.

With our deeper understanding of character, and probably some new story ideas, we can update the synopsis. It and the character profiles are working documents: they'll change as the story develops. But even something as rough as the synopsis for *The Rosie Result* that we saw in the previous chapter (now with the addition of Don's journey) is enough to allow us to move on to more deliberate generation of story.

8
Brainstorming the Story

At the end of this stage, you'll have:

1. About 180 cards, each describing a story beat
2. Updated synopsis and character profiles.

This is the 'bucket of cards' stage, where we put ideas for story beats (scenes, summaries, reflections, anything that might go in the manuscript) onto around 180 cards, without concern for sequence. It's real brainstorming stuff. Don't be put off by that big number: if you allow three months for this stage (a realistic timeframe), then two cards per day will get you there.

You don't need an actual bucket—though I do use an ice-cream container. My cards are 125 x 75 millimetre (5 x 3 inch) index cards from an office-supplies shop.

You could just type the ideas into a computer, but the cards are easy to work with in the next stage, and the bucket reinforces the attitude we want to bring to the task: fill it up with ideas without regard to sequence. It's a contrast to the linearity of the synopsis and intended to encourage the creativity that comes from looking at a problem in different ways. If you're writing memoir, the process may help you to access memories that might not have surfaced otherwise.

There are computer tools, notably Scrivener, which enable you to create electronic cards and move them around on the screen, with the advantage that you won't need to transcribe them later. You'll have to weigh the convenience of an end-to-end solution against the additional load of learning and driving it, and the accessibility of cards at any time. Even as an ex-IT guy, I'm a Luddite here.

If you'd like to take a shot at laying your story out in sequence directly, you can omit the cards and go straight to a high-level *beat sheet*—a summary of the key moments in the story:

> *Rosie gets a job in Melbourne*
> *Hudson has trouble adjusting at school*
> *Hudson has a meltdown*

You can then expand this into more detailed beats (in particular, individual scenes, as we'll discuss shortly):

> *Rosie gets an email confirming a job in Melbourne*
> *Don and Rosie move to Melbourne*
> *Don gets a call from the ski resort where Hudson is on a school excursion*
> *Don drives to the ski resort reflecting on Hudson's issues*

If, working this way, you can get to a complete story that you're happy with, congratulations! You can skip the rest of this chapter and the next. If not, you can still use whatever beats you've come up with as material for cards.

This bucket-filling can be satisfying and fun: it's where story really starts being created, and the sit-down work every day is minimal. It's a good time to do some walking or woodchopping. For an eighty-thousand-word novel, 120 final cards is about right: in the next stage you'll dump some and add new ones. I've suggested fifty per cent more, both to push you to keep thinking beyond the point where you have sufficient quantity and to give you more possibilities to choose from when you've finished.

It sounds easy, and some days it is, but you do need a certain amount of elapsed time for ideas to develop. There's a limit to how hard you can push creativity. This apparently easiest of stages is the one you're most likely to blow the schedule on—skipping days; letting 'not much to do' become 'nothing to do'; not feeling you're there yet. If that happens, you just have to accept it and keep going.

Remind yourself that the story generation that you're doing here has to be done at some point, and without this stage you'll be trying to do it as you write. Generating cards for *The Rosie Result* took six months, though I had a lot of other things happening, including another book to edit.

Unlike the drafting stage, where you'll want to be distracted as little as possible, the brainstorming stage benefits from the stimulation that comes from reading, reviewing others' writing and working on your skills.

Research

This stage is the ideal time to do research, which should inspire some cards in itself. Unless you're working in a very specialised or personal area, you're likely to find that the internet will provide most of the answers you're looking for. But I'm going to suggest that your first port of call be people—people you know or people you track down.

I know: writers are stereotypically introverts, and finding people is time-consuming. *But*, aside from the health advantages of getting out of the garret, you learn stuff—the inside dope on details, feelings, controversies—that goes beyond the official story, and will give life and authenticity to your writing. If you have friends in any vocation or pursuing a hobby, you'll have been surprised and enlightened by their unofficial takes on what goes on. That's what you want for your novel.

Visit the places where the story is set or their nearest local equivalents—or set the story in places you *can* visit. If your protagonist is a bartender, make some cocktails. If they're going to pick up a gun for the first time and shoot it, go to a shooting range and find out what it feels like.

If I want to know about autism organisations, I can read their mission statements online, but I'll learn more by having coffee informally with a few of their employees and clients. The DSM-5 diagnostic manual gave me the psychiatric profession's official view of autism, but I got a very different picture—and stories—from individual psychiatrists, psychologists and the person checking out education options for their autistic kid (that's the origin of the special-school scene in *The Rosie Result*).

The 'child killing a pigeon' idea came from a psychiatrist, and the chapter in which two autism activists clash over some of the key issues of diagnosis and treatment was an outcome of attending conferences and talking to delegates. A chat with a social worker who worked with autistic kids gave me the idea of another woman criticising Rosie for not being at home with Hudson. I paid for my own autism assessment, being honest about why I was doing it,[7] and the assessor duly shared some stories and opinions.

Structure and point of view

Before we start on the cards, there are a couple of decisions that, if taken now, can make the job easier and reduce the risk of reworking later.

The first is structure, which you should have at least thought about. You don't absolutely need to know the structure until you begin to put the cards in sequence, but if you do know it now, you'll be primed to create cards for the elements of that structure—inciting incident, turning points, climax and so on—and to flesh out the acts.

If you're considering a story that breaks naturally into, say, three to five substantial episodes (perhaps set in different times), you may want to, at least provisionally, consider them as acts—and start thinking about the turning points that will open and close each one. Or you may have identified a few major turning points already: you can, again provisionally, think of them as act breaks, and define your acts accordingly. My initial structure for *The Best of Adam Sharp* was defined this way: Part 1: 1989—Adam falls in love with Angelina. Part 2, Act 1: Present day—Adam reconnects with Angelina. Act 2: Present day: Adam progresses his relationship with Angelina. Act 3: Adam decides his future. I later refined this simple sequence, but it was a useful starting point.

If you don't have a structure in mind, I'd default to the three-act format described in Chapter 4, with the option of revising later.

The second issue is *point of view*, which might seem to be

---

[7] I went into the assessment open-minded about what the result might be. I discuss it in the previously mentioned essay 'Rewiring' in the anthology *Split*.

something we could leave until the drafting stage. But we're about to start brainstorming scenes and reflections, and need to know which of our characters will be there to describe them. If we're writing the book from the point of view of one character, they need to witness a scene for it to appear in the story in real time (as distinct from being reported by someone else to the point-of-view character).

Most novels today are written in third-person close (also called third-person limited) or in first person; in either case we are following one individual at a time, though perhaps more than one in the story as a whole. We are privy to their thoughts and observations but not to things happening outside their space.

The Rosie Result is told from the point of view of Don Tillman, so there can be no scenes in which Don is not present. If Hudson's teacher and the principal have a private conversation, we can have a scene in which Don is *told* about this conversation, but he can't witness it directly.

In *Two Steps Forward* and *Two Steps Onward*, Anne and I used alternating first-person narrators, Zoe and Martin. We could propose scenes in which either or both were present, but not scenes that neither witnessed—they could only learn about such scenes indirectly.

There are other, less commonly used options, including third-person omniscient, third-person objective (camera view, no access to thoughts), and writing from the perspective of an omniscient being such as God or someone in heaven. If you're contemplating these, you won't be restricted in your scenes.

For modern examples of the omniscient point of view, try *Beloved* by Toni Morrison, *Before You Knew My Name* by Jacqueline Bublitz and *The Book Thief* by Marcus Zusak (narrated by Death).

Or you may opt for the story to be narrated by a secondary character, which means that *they* need to be present: Watson in the Sherlock Holmes stories. As always, if you're taking the road less travelled, you should read up on the theory and check out some others' journeys to get a sense of the effect. Successful examples include *The Great Gatsby* and John Irving's *A Prayer for Owen Meany*.

These options account for the overwhelming majority of published books, but the ways to tell stories are virtually limitless—you could try a story within a story, as in John Irving's *The World According to Garp* or David Foster Wallace's *The Broom of the System*.

If in doubt, try it out. Take an event from your synopsis and experiment with writing it in the different forms under consideration. It's the quickest way to get a feeling—and it's feeling as much as anything that matters here—for the different styles as both writer and reader. At one time I attempted an objective point of view, with no access to any character's thoughts. A commonly cited example of this is Hemingway's 'Hills Like White Elephants', but every screenwriter works that way. In a novel, it wasn't as easy or effective as I thought it would be, and I gained a renewed appreciation of how important those internal worlds are to a novelist.

Types of cards: scene, summary, pause and ellipsis

To reiterate: the goal of this card-creation phase is to generate the beats that will eventually form the story, without worrying about sequence, completeness or consistency. It's authentic brainstorming—you can jump from one part of the story to another as the ideas come. You want to cover the territory defined by the synopsis, but you are not bound by it. The story is likely to change as a result of this stage, and that's fine.

The narratology theorist Gérard Genette divided narrative into four categories, using the idea of *story time* and *discourse time*:

basically, how fast our story is moving compared with the events it's describing. We can classify our cards the same way:

1. *Scene* is 'real time': dialogue and descriptions of events as they happen. As a guideline, if you can imagine it playing out on the screen, it's a scene—classic 'show, don't tell', action and dialogue. *Rosie appeared with my notebook computer.* [action] *'What do you want to say for areas you'd like to improve? I put fashion.'* [dialogue]

   Screenwriters (who are great users of cards as a tool for outlining story) define a scene more precisely as action taking place in a continuous time and place: practically, something you could film in a single shot. That's one card for them: you can be less rigid.

2. *Summary* is when we compress events, often to provide historical (background) information. *Several times he had exploded in frustration at some obstacle.* It's difficult to imagine this playing out on the screen, except perhaps as a montage.

3. *Pause* is when we stop the story to describe the scene or to present a character's reflections or our own commentary as authors. *There were two speakers. One was approximately forty…* [description] *In the adult world, an uneven distribution of abilities is more valuable than mediocrity at everything…* [Don's reflections] Again, hard to imagine these playing out on the screen—except as voiceover.

4. *Ellipsis* is when we leave the story altogether to discuss something else—to go off on a tangent that doesn't

progress the story. If we take 'progress the story' to
include 'progress character understanding', then I can't
find an example in *The Rosie Result*—you can thank
my editor for eliminating my clever asides. In *The Best
of Adam Sharp*, I had quite a long passage critiquing
a Bruce Springsteen song. One of my first readers, a
literary writer, thought it was the best passage in the
book. My editor pushed back, and that darling was also
killed ('killing darlings' refers to eliminating writing
that we may consider brilliant in itself, but which does
not advance the story).

To these we can add *sequences*, which could involve a combination
of the above. *Don travels to the ski resort to rescue Hudson*. It's a good
idea to break these down into multiple cards, especially if there is
the possibility of experimenting with their individual placement in
the story.

You don't need to label your cards with their categories, but you
should be aware of them, for one critical reason: only *scenes* deliver
'show, don't tell'. If you want to write a book that observes this
maxim (and in popular fiction, it's the way to be thinking), aim to
have mainly scenes on your cards. Remember, screenwriters generally
manage to tell their stories using only scenes. You'll find you fill in
the missing bits—particularly description and reflections—naturally
in the drafting stage.

Coming up with cards

The cards are a means to an end: a base of material that will later
be organised into an outline of your story. The only real rule is that
if you've got something that could fit into your story somewhere,

be it scene, summary, pause, ellipsis, sequence or just a half-formed idea, write it on a card.

I recommend carrying a few blank cards to fill out whenever an idea comes to you. I suggested to my memoir-writing surgeon that she begin by capturing anecdotes. But because she also had opinions she wanted to share, I proposed a second category of cards called *rants*. The pejorative name was deliberate: I was encouraging her to make her argument through examples with occasional commentary rather than the other way around. Show, don't tell.

Unless you're collaborating with someone, your cards only have to be meaningful to you, so there are no rules about format. Just keep them short and simple. Try to avoid using 'and' unless the two beats are inextricably linked—if not, break it into two cards.

I've sometimes used coloured cards for separating plot and subplot, or highlighting the scenes in which a particular character featured to ensure I didn't leave them out of the story for too long. But I usually leave this refinement till later. I didn't bother suggesting that the surgeon put her rants on different colour cards to her anecdotes: I just wanted her to get her ideas down. If you decide later to colour code, you can copy the existing cards, which will encourage you to review them. Cards are cheap.

Use the reverse sides of the cards for notes: location, characters, *any* ideas you have for that beat that might be useful when you come to write it. If you run out of space on the card, write it in the synopsis—or in your notebook or on another card. Don't throw away anything and don't trust to memory.

Your first few cards will come easily but it gets harder. You're trying to come up with everything you want to happen in your story, not just fill a bucket. The good news is that a single idea frequently leads to several beats to set it up and play it out. As you identify these, you'll be building connections between the cards—cohesion for your story.

Here are twelve stimuli for coming up with cards. I suggest you start at the top and run with that technique for as long as it's productive, then move on the next. And then return to the beginning. Ultimately, we'll want each of our written beats to advance story and character, but if you have an idea for something that doesn't fill those criteria, put it on a card. Give yourself plenty to work with rather than being too selective at this stage.

1. If you've begun drafting your novel already, reverse-engineer the cards: identify scenes or other substantial passages in the text and make a card for each. Your work hasn't been wasted, and this stage is going to help you incorporate it into a bigger picture. I've worked with authors who have multiple pieces of writing intended for the same project, but which are otherwise only loosely connected. Great material for cards, and this exercise allowed them to fill the gaps—creating the missing story components. Likewise, if you've attempted but not completed a beat sheet, then the beats you've got will suggest scenes and sequences.

2. The synopsis is a natural starting point, and will yield some quick and important beats:
    School asks for autism assessment
    Don quits job
    Don teaches Hudson life skills (generated several cards as
       I brainstormed the skills)

3. If your synopsis doesn't include the key elements of your intended structure, create cards for them, even if they're just

placeholders or dummies. When I was working on *The Rosie Effect*, I had a first-act-turning-point card that read *Don gets into trouble for something* and a second-act-turning-point card that read *Everything goes to shit*. I should have done more work on that synopsis, but inspiration will come once you've identified the need and started thinking about it.

4. You'll likely find it hardest to generate enough beats for the main journey (the second act in a three-act structure). Breaking it into two or more phases can help. At the midpoint of *The Rosie Result* (which splits the second act into two parts) Don enlists his friends to help Hudson with social skills, so we have two stimuli for cards: Don helping Hudson and Don's friends helping Hudson.

    Look for obstacles to place between the protagonist and his or her goal(s) as they change though the story. For most conventional stories, the work of overcoming these obstacles is going to provide the bulk of the narrative. Put yourself in the shoes of those who would frustrate our protagonist: make these antagonists as determined and inventive as your imagination will allow.

    Storytelling convention allows acts of God to get in the way of the protagonist—but not so much to help them, and certainly not to provide their ultimate victory. That's *deus ex machina*—from the Greek dramatic convention of the gods stepping in to save the day. It's unsatisfying to readers, who want to see the protagonist triumph through their own efforts, rather than by good luck. Nor do they want the protagonist to wake and find it was all a dream.

5. Create necessary set-ups and consequences. Some scenes or

sequences (in particular, the climax) are going to emerge as set pieces—substantial, often extended, scenes that the reader will experience as highlights. If they are to be believable and have the impact you want, they need to be well set up: much of the story will be about putting in place the necessary people, motivations and circumstances.

Those set-up scenes have to earn their place by being relevant and dramatic in their own right, rather than just signalling to the reader what is to come.

In *The Rosie Result*, I wanted to showcase Don's family of origin and needed to give him a reason to visit them regularly (having previously established that he wasn't the most attentive of sons). My solution was that his father should be dying. That gave me two cards at least:

Don's father is ill. (That's not a beat yet, just a placeholder.)

Don's father dies. (That's definitely a scene / sequence and potentially a big, emotional one.)

If the death of our protagonist's father is to be a powerful moment for the reader, they need to get to know him first—in a few scenes that not only showcase his character but advance the story:

Don's reflects on his father's illness. (Or discusses it? Or argues with Rosie about visiting him?)

Don's father demonstrates how he 'coached' Don as a child.

Don's father explains his Beethoven project. (He's listening to every work of Beethoven before he dies—we get to see the similarity between him and Don.)

Don's father asks Don to get Beethoven's final symphony for him. (Don's mother has held it back, believing he'll die when he's heard the last one.)

The Beethoven idea had generated material for a little, but significant, subplot that needed to be resolved. *Don plays Beethoven's Ninth Symphony for his father*. The reader can see what's about to happen now. So, I reversed it, or at least added another beat of tension. *Don's father doesn't die*; *Don's father asks Don to play the Moonlight Sonata*. And finally…well, we've already got the pay-off card: *Don's father dies*.

Now the consequences: *Don's father's funeral*. This was a dummy card until I could come up with something that progressed the story. It later became *At his father's funeral, Don learns how his father tried to help Don fit in*. And I got a bunch of cards from thinking about the events that might follow a death. *Don is shocked when his mother announces she's selling the family home*. It's line ball whether this progresses the story, but it contradicts Don's supposed separation from family and gives us a chance for his mother to play a bigger role. When in doubt (at this brainstorming stage), leave it in.

6. Check the character profiles for their individual journeys and the events they participate in. Is there a powerful / memorable way of introducing them? Don first encounters Blue House Fan as an obnoxious voice behind him at the school swimming carnival. Later, he hears that same voice again and realises that the man is Blanche's father (and the reader, along with Don, instantly knows a lot about him as they make the connection). And we can arouse a little curiosity through the man being known only by his voice.

7. Look for the interaction of characters with the main plot. Who should be there? What will they bring? Does it need to be set up? Once I'd established that Don would enlist his

friends to help Hudson, I could ask: what would George the Drummer do to help? No-brainer—teach Hudson to play drums. Perhaps Hudson wouldn't let on that he was learning. And Phil the Footballer? Football. But let's subvert that. Maybe Phil teaches him to play chess instead, sharing his hard-earned wisdom that intellectual growth is more important than sporting prowess. Once you connect interesting characters with plot and a dash of creative thinking, story will come.

8. Don't forget the subplots, if you have them. Again, use dummy cards as temporary placeholders if necessary, until you can work out the details. *Rosie has a problem at work; Rosie's work problem becomes serious; Rosie triumphs at work.*

9. Look for external events that may intersect with the story. A global occasion like Christmas can generate scenes—just pull the family together and watch the action unfold. Then there will be events relevant to the setting and genre: every crime investigation, love story or physical journey has certain milestones. In *The Rosie Effect*, the pregnancy prompted cards for the test result, the ultrasound and the antenatal class (not to mention the birth), all of which Don would respond to in his characteristic way.

In the case of *The Rosie Result*, I had the school calendar to play with. Sports days offered opportunities to show Hudson's progress or lack of it. Sex-education evening had comedic possibilities. Graduation night struck me as a powerful setting for Hudson to come out as autistic in front of all the characters—public drama almost always being more powerful than private.

10. Not for the last time, I'll draw your attention to the rule of three. There's a storytelling convention, epitomised by the three people who walk into a bar, in which a situation is set up in two story beats, then paid off in the third. For something as big as Don's father's death, we may have more than two set-up beats, but if we want a scene to hit home—or, in some cases, be credible—it will generally benefit from having at least two.

> *Don reconnects with his friend George the Drummer, seeking advice on Hudson—George is sympathetic to Hudson's plight.*
>
> *Hudson tells off Don for not keeping in touch with George (revealing that he—Hudson—is in contact with him).*
>
> Pay-off: *George incites Don to deal with Gary after turning up at Hudson's graduation to see him perform on drums.*

That's two set-up cards in addition to the pay-off beat, which is stronger and more credible for having been set up (George has a reason to fly in for the graduation).

11. Use the Hero's Journey and other templates (see Chapter 4) to prompt scenes. You can cherrypick and adapt ideas from any of them without signing up to their structure. *Save the Cat!*'s template begins with *opening image*, a very filmic concept. But novels can be visual too. Is there an opening scene that gives us a taste of what's to come? Can we make it strikingly visual? Can we create an image capturing the essence of our protagonist, their world, their predicament?

The Rosie Result originally began with Don reflecting on his problems. But the opening-image idea prompted me to rethink it. So now it's Don shucking oysters in his pyjamas while doing single-leg dips. As he narrates (which gives us his voice), we see his disregard for convention, his concern with fitness, his utter confidence that his approach is right. Metaphorically, I wanted to set up the story with Don confidently trying to do something and coming unstuck.

Because we are not constrained to the visual, we can extend the idea. Could there be an opening smell or sound or taste or physical sensation? Adam Sharp opens by invoking the song 'Hey Jude' as a metaphor for his life.

In his Hero's Journey, Joseph Campbell gives us a beat called *Meeting with the Mentor*. It led me to the idea of Don, faced with trouble, calling up his friends for advice—a chance to (re)introduce them to the reader and canvass different options for dealing with his problem with Hudson. Six friends, six scenes, six cards. Easy, though I then had to work out how each one would advance Don's thinking and the story as a whole. Ultimately, I discarded one, and the remaining five cards gave me a full chapter.

Since Hudson has his own significant journey in the story, I went back to the Hero's Journey with him in mind. This time, *Meeting with the Mentor* suggested Hudson might find his own mentor, without Don knowing—I ended up choosing his grandfather and creating scenes to show how that played out. Later, Don's friend Dave steps into that role.

Master of Both Worlds and *Freedom to Live,* the final steps in the Hero's Journey, suggested Hudson having the option of choosing either the high school or the special school and having achieved some level of independence.

12. Occasionally, take the cards out of the bucket, put them
    in rough story order (as described in the next section), cull
    duplicates and those that no longer work for you, and look for
    gaps, set-ups and consequences.

So: think laterally, cast the net wide, do whatever it takes to create
cards. The above prompts can help, but some of the work is just down
to the creative magic of 'finding story' (that's an intimidating term:
'inventing beats' seems easier). At least we're not trying to come up
with major characters, define an overall plot and write scintillating
prose at the same time.

Anne and I spent a year brainstorming our novel set in a mental-
health facility—a background activity while we were involved in other
projects. When we decided to get more serious, on a three-month
road trip, we struggled and eventually put the forty cards we'd come
up with aside. Then the creative incubation period did its magic.
When we revisited the story, some months later, we had a full set
of cards in two days.

At this point in *The Rosie Result*, I had 150 scene cards and
thirty-nine 'other' cards—rants and half-baked ideas. They proved
sufficient for moving to the next step.

Organising the cards—first cut

When you have your target number of cards (by default, 180) *and*
you're out of ideas (meaning you've done a week or so of working
at it without feeling you've added anything worthwhile), it's time
to empty the bucket.

Find yourself a large space to lay out the cards—I use the floor—
and sort them into the order in which you plan to tell the story. If you
haven't decided that yet, put the cards in chronological order of story

events. You'll probably be surprised at how much choice you have about the sequence of events and the order in which they appear in the book. Don't sweat it too much (you'll do that in the next stage).

Give yourself a few days with the cards laid out (you can pack them up into a deck, in order, and lay them out again if others have to use that floor in between times). Take the opportunity to do a bit of cleaning up. You'll likely find cards that were the result of a wild idea you've already abandoned, duplicates, and cards you wrote in desperation to complete your daily target. They can go.

Cards that are 'just' ideas rather than real story beats should be translated into scenes or other passages if possible—the rest can be put aside. And in doing all this, perhaps you'll be inspired to create a few more.

You should have a sense of a story emerging, albeit still with some holes. Do your best to fill them. In the case of *The Rosie Result*, I ended up with 146 cards and the confidence that I had a detailed foundation for a book.

Review your synopsis and character profiles. It's likely there will be changes as a result of the work you've done in this stage.

In the next two stages, we'll continue to review and develop our card-based outline. The more you do now, the less you'll have to do then.

9

Organising the Story

At the end of this stage, you'll have:

1. A draft story outline
2. Revised synopsis and character profiles.

If you've done a solid job of generating cards, this stage is going to be rewarding. With your story literally laid out, you'll be able to experiment with different ways of telling it. And you'll begin to get a sense of the finished manuscript's shape.

Structure

If you haven't decided on a structure, you should do so now, understanding that you can change it if it isn't working. For simplicity, I'm going to assume that you'll be running with three acts, including a midpoint, but it's straightforward to adapt what I'm saying to other structures. Even something like 'A series of meditations on diverse topics', which might sound hopelessly vague or even *anti*-structure, is fine to work with: the division into meditations creates a quite strict and granular structure, and you'll have plenty to do fitting the cards into their appropriate meditations and sequencing them for best effect.

In *The Best of Adam Sharp*, I found the three-act structure wasn't working, and opted instead to organise the book into two parts. The first part became a three-act love story that had taken place twenty-two years earlier told in analepsis (flashbacks) against a present-day narrative of the couple reconnecting. The second part was also in three acts, but the first act (set-up) was shorter than normal, much of it having already been covered in Part 1. Complicated? A bit. But I had reasons (I discuss one of them below), and once I had articulated what I was doing, it was not much harder than working with a three-act structure.

Laying out your story

Let's get organised. I take four cards of a colour I haven't used yet and mark them Act 1, Act 2a, Act 2b and Act 3 (as I said before, you could call it a four-act structure, but these are the conventions). I place them on the floor to mark the start of the relevant acts. Then I do my best to put my cards first into their acts and then into the order they will appear in the finished novel.

Ultimately, we want the four parts to be of roughly the same length. Different cards will generate different amounts of prose, but the number of them in each part is a good preliminary indication of how you're doing.

As for sequence, readers are used to stories being told out of chronological order. They're accustomed to analepsis, in particular. But you should have a reason for playing with the timeline. There are plenty, and the three-act structure does not restrict you: what it specifies is the shape of the *story*—as told or revealed by you—rather than the timeline of the events it chronicles.

Act 1 might be set in the present day, but at the first-act turning point the narrator could reveal that the current situation is the result of a dramatic series of past events. Act 2 might go back in time to describe those events and Act 3 could return to the present to show how the protagonist deals with them.

Sometimes our first reason for departing from chronological sequence is to open the story with a powerful passage that will pull the reader in and *foreshadow* what is to come, perhaps encouraging them to tolerate some less dramatic but essential set-up while they're waiting to discover the outcome.

If you're writing a memoir, it's worth looking for such a strong moment; once it's in place at the opening, other scenes may naturally follow. Keith Richards' autobiography, *Life*, opens with him being pulled over in the US with a carload of illegal drugs. We read on because he and his companions are in jeopardy, and we want to see how it turns out.

If this is your first book, the advice to open dramatically goes double. Established authors may be cut a little slack; you want that acquisitions editor and other readers meeting you for the first time to be riveted from the get-go.

Similarly, it's good to get your main characters into the story early. There's a rule of thumb in screenwriting that if an audience doesn't meet a character in the first ten minutes (roughly the first ten per cent of the story), they won't care much about them.

I turned this advice on its head in *The Rosie Project*, holding back Rosie's entry into the story so that readers (especially those female readers who might instinctively side with the woman in a straight romantic comedy) *wouldn't* identify with her but would instead join Don on his journey.

In *The Best of Adam Sharp*, I wanted the reader to meet Adam's present partner and his long-lost lover early, so they would be on reasonably equal terms in the reader's mind. I began in the present day, but then alternated between that time and twenty years earlier. By the midpoint of the story, I was in the present, with just occasional flashbacks to other events in Adam's life.

If your setting or 'world' is unusual in some way that's important to the story (e.g. magic is possible, the hero has superpowers, technology has advanced), you should set up the rules (generally by demonstration: show, don't tell) before you start using them to drive story, and especially to get the hero out of trouble, or the reader will feel cheated.

So, play with the sequence. Remember, you can control both the order of events as they would play out in real life and the order in which you're narrating them. Some events are locked into sequence by cause and effect, but you'll be surprised at how many are not. *Don meets Hudson's friend Blanche. Rosie complains about her boss's sexism. Visits to Don's parents.* I had quite a bit of choice about where I placed these scenes.

Even in a story that was told largely in chronological order, I had a few flashbacks, notably a full chapter devoted to Don getting into trouble at work, presented after the resulting disciplinary hearing had been mentioned.

But be bold. Try things out. You're just moving cards around. Take photos or list the cards if you're afraid you'll forget a promising option.

Reviewing the acts

Once you've got your cards organised into acts, the anomalies will stand out. The most common of these is a disproportionately large number of cards in Act 1. Too much set-up. And the second most common: not enough cards in Act 3. Insufficient story.

My rough goal for an eighty-thousand-word novel is thirty cards per quarter. True to expectations, my card distribution for *The Rosie Result* looked like this:

Act 1: 50
Act 2a: 39
Act 2b: 31
Act 3: 27

For Act 1, in the unlikely event that you have too few cards, it's probably because you don't really *have* a first act. It's not enough to set up the background: you want to get a story moving—a dramatic question posed, some drama happening—before the first-act turning point sets it off in another direction.

Reviewing the first act

For a while I thought that Don's decision in *The Rosie Result* to quit his job would be his immediate response to the inciting incident of Hudson's school requesting an autism assessment. In that case, I'd have had the 'short Act 1' problem. But I was able to frame the first act as Don searching for solutions to a host of problems, adding the drama of these (Hudson's school excursion, Don's ill-fated lecture and so on) to the mix. His cut-through decision marked the end of that quest and the beginning of the next: to coach Hudson.

By then, I was in the usual predicament—too many cards. Best to think of it as having an embarrassment of riches.

You can do at least four things to address your card surplus: eliminate, consolidate, abbreviate or move them to the second act.

Or live with a longer first act, and the risk that your readers will get impatient about where the story is going.

At the first pass, ask yourself—for each card—do we need this? Will the story work without it? All beats should meet the basic criteria of progressing story and / or developing character, but that's not the same as saying they're essential. This is not the last time you may have to 'kill your darlings' but it's seldom as bad as it sounds. If you have a scene that's particularly powerful or moving or hilarious, you can favour that over others that are less so.

Often we can incorporate the job that a card is doing (particularly when it's only developing character) into another beat. A line of dialogue elsewhere can summarise what was played out on the original card.

There are often opportunities to cut the number of cards in a sequence (do we need to know about Don preparing for his lecture or debriefing with his boss afterwards?). Readers, accustomed to the shorthand of film and television, don't need to be told about things that they can easily figure out must have happened or will happen. If you're uncertain about removing a card, set it aside in a pile labelled 'outtakes' that you may reinstate (you won't, but it will stop you fretting).

The likely candidates for moving to the second act include the beginnings of any subplots. It's natural to want to get everything set up in the first act, but subplots can usually wait till early in the second.

Reviewing the second act

The problem with the second act is usually the opposite to that with the first: not enough story. It's the longest act—half the book. If you break it in two with a midpoint, the problem is less daunting: you now have two stories to flesh out, but they're each only half the size of the full act. If you have subplots, they will fill some gaps, but beware of adding too many or too much to compensate for a main story that isn't big enough.

Your cue to generating more story is the description given to the second act: *complications arise.* What additional challenges or obstacles can we throw at our protagonists? You tried to do this when you generated cards: it's time to do it again, this time with the cards laid out so you can see the flow and gaps visually. Try looking at each card and asking: what's the worst thing that could happen to the protagonists now?

Once we have enough story, we may still be left with a problem— one that, in my experience, is the single most common fault in novels. It's so common that it has more than one name: *the hole in the second act* or *the mushy middle.* They describe the symptom: a feeling on the part of the reader and sometimes the writer that the story has lost pace and direction.

The cause is usually a lack of escalation. Readers expect the stakes and challenges to get bigger: it's a storytelling convention, though not an accurate reflection of real life. Hence the problem. Our story may be true to life, but it's boring.

In the real world, if we're faced with a series of challenges, they're unlikely to present themselves in increasing order of difficulty. If we know what they are in advance, we might well choose to tackle the most difficult or dangerous one first while we're in good shape: get it done and the rest will be easy. Smart thinking, except that when we write about it, our readers will give up at that point, knowing we have it sorted.

Readers expect the opposite approach: start with the (relatively) easy stuff, and build up competence and confidence as we move forward. And they expect the universe to co-operate in throwing up ever more challenging obstacles.

Adding a midpoint gives you a chance for a reset, and to start again with a new goal and (initially) easier obstacles. Regardless, you have two basic strategies to deal with an escalation problem:

1. Reorder the events so that the easier, less-dramatic challenges come first: Hudson learning to catch a ball is lower-key than learning to ride a bike, which Don is also emotionally invested in. The swimming carnival, where Hudson is set up for public humiliation, takes us to another level. The need for escalation drove my ordering of those story beats.

2. Raise the stakes and difficulty of the later events. (You could lower the stakes of the earlier ones, but let's aim for more drama, rather than less.) In Act 2b, Hudson is in trouble for allegedly killing a pigeon: it's the final escalation, and I made it as strong as I could by tying it not only to his acceptance into high school, but to his relationship with his best friend, who has informed on him. And to his trust in Don to see him through. And to his mental health: at this point I wanted readers to be really concerned for this eleven-year-old. It's a long way from not being able to catch a ball.

Is it only in the second act that we want escalation? No, we want it in every act—but it tends to happen more naturally in the first and third as we, respectively, build up a story and hurtle toward its climax. You shouldn't move on from this stage until you're satisfied that every act has escalation (or, as you're always free to do, you've made a conscious, informed decision to break with convention).

Now that I've hammered home the importance of escalation, in the context of obstacles, I'm going to suggest a bit of the opposite—not so much de-escalation, but punctuation. The tendency, reinforced by such models as the Hero's Journey, is to focus on the tough and unpleasant: the eleven-year-old betrayed and his parents bereft. We need light and shade (believe it or not at this point, *The Rosie Result* is a comedy, though that's more a result of tone).

In *The Bestseller Code: Anatomy of the Blockbuster Novel*, published in 2016, Jodie Archer and Matthew L. Jockers analysed recent *New York Times* bestsellers, and concluded that the balance of emotional highs and lows was an important contributor to success. I was pleased to see *The Rosie Project* cited near the top of the list. On the face of it, this is a story of setback after setback as our man pursues his goal of finding a life partner, but there are interludes when he's winning not only in the romantic stakes, but in taking down his adversaries and overcoming his own issues. These are invariably the passages that my readers tell me are their favourites (the cocktail sequence is the popular choice).

Contrary to what some might expect, the big emotional moments—the ones that bring tears to a reader's eyes—come more often from acts of kindness and happiness than cruelty and suffering. And, as one agent put it, *they cry, they buy*.

Against the odds, Hudson wins the swimming race in *The Rosie Result*; after Don embarrasses himself at the sex-education evening, he's hailed for his bravery in speaking out; when Hudson is suspended from school, Don takes him on a male-bonding fishing weekend with his buddy Dave. Of course, we may be planning for all to turn out right at the climax, but we want some moments along the way too. Think of it as our protagonists taking a break in the valley before tackling the next mountain, and use the opportunity to show them enjoying themselves.

Reviewing the third act

The third act is often short on cards, and I can almost guarantee that if you don't fix the problem, your editors and readers will tell you that the ending was 'rushed'. It's tough, because you *want* the pace to have picked up in this act. So more has to happen: more twists and turns and escalation.

My first tactic is to look for a 'false climax'. We could have tried to create one while we were brainstorming cards, but the opportunity usually presents itself now (or later), when the story has more shape. We're aiming for a beat that appears to be the climax but will later be reversed and / or trumped. That might mean adding it in before the real climax, or, more satisfying and actually more often, relegating your planned climax to 'false climax' and writing a new climax that takes the story to another level.

Hercules completes his ten labours: job done, feels like the climax. Then King Eurystheus disqualifies two and replaces them with two more, now aware of what Hercules is capable of. We're back in the story and the final labour is unsurprisingly the toughest.

Alternatively, our hero fails—but then finds a way to give it one more try. In *The Rosie Project*, I originally concluded with Don's proposal of marriage being accepted. But then I turned it around: Rosie rejects him, and it's only after a 'dark night of the soul' (another common beat in generic structures) that he finds a way through to an even bigger climax, featuring most of the main characters in the story. If you find yourself doing this—adding on another tilt at the prize—you may have originally set up the false ending so effectively that readers will believe the hero has been defeated, a powerful emotional moment before the ultimate high, or even the ultimate failure.

Or the hero achieves their external goal, but not the deeper goal, which becomes the subject of the real climax. *Hudson is allowed into the mainstream high school.* But later: *Hudson rejects the offer and announces he'll attend the special school, where he'll be accepted for himself.*

The added ending (or inserted false ending) is seldom just one beat, but a series of scenes, set-ups and consequences that are likely to give you the cards you're missing. Try hard to find it.

Check also that subplots are resolved and character arcs completed—somewhere in the story, but usually toward the end. You don't *have* to resolve anything but if you decide to leave something open, it should be a conscious decision rather than an oversight. Often there's an opportunity to bring a character back as the climax approaches and their presence may inspire story (George the Drummer flies in for Hudson's graduation and plays a key role in Don's fight with Gary the Homeopath).

Work at this until you're looking at around twenty-five to thirty cards for each of Acts 1, 2a, 2b and 3—or are happy to break the rules.

Reviewing the full story
Now, laid out in front of you, is your story. Take a look at it as a whole.

1. You may already have spotted some plot problems. One of the negatives of non-linear brainstorming is that you can end up with continuity issues; a card that looked good in isolation turns out not to work in the bigger story. The story has to be credible, at least within the world you've set up. There's

no universal answer to such problems, but I suggest you focus
initially on defining the issue as clearly as you can—perhaps
explain it to someone else. Sometimes that's enough to suggest
an answer. Otherwise, reserve creative time for it.

2. For each card, ask: at this point, what dramatic questions are
    in play? The big dramatic questions are our fallback position,
    but we should be raising questions that the reader is looking
    forward to having answered in the meantime, perhaps in the
    next page or two (*Will Don get to open his bar? Will Hudson
    be exonerated for the pigeon killing? Will Don win the fight?*).
    What, besides our deathless prose, will motivate the reader
    to keep reading, right now? We're looking for conflict,
    jeopardy or simple curiosity—perhaps as simple as a passing
    reference to some previously unknown fact that piques the
    reader's curiosity: *The only significant blemish was the loss of my
    longstanding friendship with my mentor, Gene.*

3. Do we have overall escalation in each of the acts, punctuated
    by ups and downs? Can we amplify these?

4. Check for rule-of-three set-ups, especially for the big scenes.
    Hudson's cross-country sports triumph was preceded by a
    couple of beats of build-up (training, planning tactics), so the
    reader would realise how important it was going to be and be
    able to assess his chances.

5. Are we meeting our main characters in good time (by halfway
    through the first act)?

6. Do all of the characters have complete arcs? (Not essential
    for minor characters, but it's worth checking for
    opportunities.)

Now I want you to tell your story, aloud, preferably to one or two trusted friends or writing-group associates. They don't have to be writers, just people who are excited about sharing in the act of creation and perhaps looking forward to seeing their names in the acknowledgments.

Turn on your voice recorder. Tell the story as well as you can, from the cards, fleshing it out as you go and stating aloud any ideas that come up: 'notes to self'. Ask your audience to take notes too but to interrupt only if they're genuinely lost. Stop after every quarter or act to debrief, making notes.

If you can, leave a day—or at least an hour or two—between quarters while you review the notes and update your cards (back and front). It's likely you'll have found holes and opportunities, so do what needs to be done.

Collect your audience's notes. You don't actually need to play back the recording except to retrieve your verbal notes if you can't remember them. Thank your collaborators profusely and buy them a drink or make them a cheesecake.

This is your last chance with the cards. Make sure you're happy. It's easier to shuffle cards around than to resequence a written story and fix the continuity errors that will arise.

Now open a new document on your computer. If you were a screenwriter, you'd call it *Scene Breakdown*, but *Outline* is fine, especially as some of your beats may be summary, pause and ellipsis, rather than actual scenes.

Transcribe the cards, in order, into the document, tidying up and improving the wording as you go and including any notes or ideas that arise. Break complex beats into multiple beats. It's a hangover from screenwriting, but I include location:

At public pool (school swimming competition), Hudson surprises
everyone by triumphing (note: parent-from-hell Gary is
criticising him)

At public pool, Phil admits to coaching Hudson secretly

At home, family celebrates Hudson's win (Don invites Dave over?)

At home, Hudson notes that Don is more excited by his sporting
win than by his academic achievement

At home, Hudson sympathises with kid he beat, whose parents
are overly ambitious

Note the turning points and any changes in the dramatic question (which typically happen at turning points).

Pack up the cards. The shaping is done. Update your synopsis and character arcs with any changes that have arisen from all this work.

Now we're going to review each beat in the story. When we've done that, we'll be ready to write.

10
Reviewing the Outline

At the end of this stage, you'll have:

1. A revised ('final') outline
2. Updated synopsis and character profiles.

We could start drafting the manuscript now, but if we want to make our job as easy—and the result as good—as possible, we do as much in advance as we can. The focus is on ensuring that each beat (I'll call them beats rather than cards—we're done with cards) contributes to the story and does so in a compelling way. But it's also an opportunity to add detail: elements of description, participants in a scene, lines of dialogue. It's all about giving yourself a flying start in translating your outline into prose.

This is a short chapter: a list of things to check for each of your beats, or at least those that will translate into scenes—or summaries. Of course you'll check beats that aren't scenes as well, but the checklist is focused on the unfolding action.

For every beat we need to ask: what purpose does this serve?

In popular fiction, we're looking to advance story and / or develop character. I'm even wary of beats that only do the second of these: it's usually possible to show character in the context of action that's relevant to the plot.

As for beats that do neither, Elmore Leonard said, 'Try to *leave out* the part that readers tend to skip.' If the beat is there purely to show off the beauty of your writing, it had better *be* beautiful, because that's all you've got to hold the reader.

Likewise, if you want to share an observation or anecdote that's peripheral to the story, it had better be captivating. And if you do too much of either, you'll literally lose the plot, and very likely at least the non-literary reader.

But now to scenes. What makes a good one? Here's my checklist:

1. The scene, or the sequence to which it belongs, should be a little story in itself (or amenable to being turned into one when you write it), not just 'one damn thing after the other'. Imagine yourself telling that story as an anecdote, with set-up, (possibly) complications and some form of completion which may raise new questions. For example, Don visits Blanche's home (set-up); interacts with Blanche's mother, which angers her father (complications); then leaves when he discovers that Blanche's father is the guy who abused him at the school sports day (completion, leaving open how Don will deal with the revelation).

    Generally, you only want to tell one story per scene. There's a temptation to use conversations as 'exposition dumps', bringing the reader up to date on several story strands. It tends to make for boring reading. This is different from having a scene that works on multiple levels through subtext: a good thing. (Don, Dave and Hudson are talking about fishing, but they—and readers—are also learning about Hudson's struggles and establishing Dave as a mentor.)

2. Show, don't tell, again. Is this a genuine scene (playing out in real time) or a summary of what happened or is happening? It's much harder to deliver conflict, drama, suspense, character and comedy in a summary. Some authors can pull it off, and we do want variation in the narrative, but writing teachers will tell you that the most common fault they see in manuscripts is too much summary and not enough scene.

   My first novel was initially written as a screenplay, so it was all scene. As I rewrote it in the new form, I deliberately introduced a bit of variation—some summary to balance the scenes. My editor then picked up almost every example: could we show rather than tell this? Fortunately, it wasn't hard to fix!

   One of my writing mentees used to complain that I was asking them to tighten their prose at the same time as replacing summary with scene. 'Summary is obviously going to take fewer words.' Not always so, despite the implication of the word 'summary'. Often what we're doing with scene is *instantiating*: showing a single instance that the reader can deduce is part of a pattern. If necessary, we can add something brief to confirm that. Rather than summarise our hero's overall experience of being bullied constantly at school (*Over the next year, there was this bully who never let up...*), let's see them walking into the classroom—where the bully is waiting. Tension, drama, action, emotion. And at the end, our hero can tell us in four words: 'He / she never let up'. Or not, if we've written the scene well enough to make that clear.

3. Something should change—be different at the end of the scene
    than it was at the beginning. It may be tangible (Don's father
    is dead), emotional (Rosie is furious at her boss), a change in
    what is known and / or how it's interpreted (Don realises that
    Blanche's father and Blue House Fan are the same person).

    This is another way of checking that the scene advances
    story or character, but it's also a cue to incorporate *reversals*,
    one of the key elements of storytelling. We've already
    encountered them in the form of turning points, where the
    story as a whole changes direction, but they're also important
    at the scene level. We go in expecting one thing, but something
    different happens, perhaps several times over.

    Reversals are the stock-in-trade of thrillers: the
    protagonist suddenly in danger, then out of it, then in it again,
    in ways we hadn't predicted. And of comedies: 'I will never,
    ever date that loser again.' Cut to the restaurant.

4. There should be conflict and / or jeopardy—most of the time, at
    least. Drama is rooted in conflict. The screenwriting guru Syd
    Field said: 'Without conflict, you have no action; without action,
    you have no character; without character, you have no story; and
    without story, you have no screenplay.' I remember reading that
    and thinking it was far too strong. But as I've written, across
    screenplays, novels, short stories and the occasional short play,
    I've found that the spirit of what he said is true. I'm not saying
    that *every* scene should have conflict—you want light and shade
    and occasional unalloyed joy—but you're more likely to run
    into trouble with lack of conflict than with too much.

    The conflict can be between characters with different

objectives or it can be internal: within a single character's mind as they try to choose between alternatives ('what should I do?'). Don pondering whether he should plead 'Asperger's syndrome' as mitigation for his lecture debacle is a one-person beat, but full of conflict.

It doesn't have to be pistols drawn, either: it could be subtext in a tender scene between two lovers who have different ideas about the future of the relationship.

Conflict is particularly helpful if you need to communicate a lot of information. Show-don't-tell isn't enough by itself to keep the reader interested. With conflict, we can have characters say things that are already known to them: *You lied to me!* (They both know it's true, but anger makes it realistic.)

In *The Rosie Result*, I had a problem scene: *Don researches current thinking on autism*. I needed Don to investigate autism to advance the story, but I couldn't have created a drier, more boring scene if I'd tried. Don in a library, telling Rosie what he's read, with Rosie listening attentively. I tried to add conflict— Rosie arguing with some of the research—and it was a little better, but only a little. So I reinvented the scene as a conflict between two passionate autism advocates, and it came alive, to the extent that it's the passage I most often read at book events.

5. Closely related to conflict is *jeopardy*: they serve the same purpose of creating drama and keeping the reader engaged. When I was writing *The Rosie Effect*, I had a scene: *Dave introduces Don to George the British rock star*. Its purpose was to set up Don taking residence in the apartment below George to maintain his beer cellar, which Dave had constructed. George was an interesting guy with an eccentric approach to

his apartment and beer. The scene should have been at least entertaining. It was notably boring. Why? No conflict, no jeopardy. No risk to Don or Dave. All I did to fix it was add a goal: Dave is there to collect payment from George and is afraid he won't pay up. Now he has a reason to bring Don, and we have jeopardy—and a set-up for conflict. Dave hates confrontation; Don is famously tactless. What's going to happen? The scene writes itself from there. (George turns out to be a pussycat—a reversal—so there's no actual conflict.)

6. We'd like at least some scenes to prompt the reader to think or feel differently about the world—be it a different perspective on autism or a new way of looking at love.

7. All the above ideas can contribute to a scene being engaging— and that is our bottom line. Is this going to be an entertaining scene to read—a scene that the reader is pulled into, as vicarious participant or fascinated observer?

8. We want to ensure the reader has a reason to keep reading, preferably in addition to the overarching dramatic question.

9. We'd like it to be well-written—indeed, beautifully written *in the context of what the story is trying to achieve* (in the Rosie series, maintaining Don's voice was more important to me than being poetic). That's a goal for the drafting and rewriting stages, but you can make notes now that will help you: anything you can think of.

That's it. Check every beat against the list. Update the synopsis and character profiles again. Give it all another hard look, and leave it for at least a few days for final ideas to incubate. Because this is the outline from which you'll be writing your novel or memoir.

11
First Draft—Process

At the end of this stage, you'll have:

1. A complete draft of your novel / memoir
2. An updated outline.

After all this planning and brainstorming and shaping, you're finally ready to start writing. If you've followed the process, you'll be working from an outline that tells a coherent story in either an established form or one of your considered choosing, supported by a synopsis and character profiles.

Your outline will have broken the story into around 120 beats— key events or scenes. For a typical novel of eighty thousand words, that's about 700 words per beat. By the time you fill in description, reflections and plot details you think of along the way, it should work out about right. One beat at a time, one day at a time, you'll write this thing. If you were a hardcore pantser, you'd be starting here, without all that planning and an outline to guide you.

We'll cover the writing of the first draft in two chapters. In this one, I'm going to discuss process (the focus of this book), including how to organise your writing day. In the next, we'll look at content—guidelines for good writing—and I won't have so much to say, relatively speaking. You'll have no trouble finding advice on that topic.

This is an exciting time. You're actually writing your book, and you're likely to be making good progress. After a few days, a chapter finished. Then another, then the end of the first act—a quarter of the way. Milestones. The work can go surprisingly quickly: three of my books took me less than a month to draft.

I'm often asked: what is your writing routine? Do you have a special place to write? And I'm usually a little dismissive. In my previous jobs, nobody asked if I had a special place to design databases or write reports. As for routine, you showed up to work and got on with it. But that first draft of a book is different.

It feels more intense than the other stages, and you're likely to become immersed in it. Take precautions to see that the rest of your life doesn't suffer unduly: thanks to having a plan, you can tell your loved ones that there's an end date, or at least an end in sight, and report on progress toward it.

You want to do all you can to maintain momentum and creativity. Quality can come third, for the moment. I like to move quickly, knowing I can tidy up later, while still striving to do the best job I can. A short timeframe helps me keep the totality of what I'm doing in my head and makes it easier to be consistent with details, such as the voices of secondary characters.

I usually travel a lot, and do my planning and rewriting wherever I happen to be, but I try to sit in one place with as few distractions as possible for a first draft. If you have a day job, you might think about taking time off, with reasonable confidence you'll be productive.

Otherwise, try hard to set aside time every day to write.

I find it helpful for motivation and planning to set a daily word target. But if you're not working to a deadline, you can just write until you run out of time or energy. What's important to me is that I don't feel pressured, so I set my target to be comfortably achievable. In fact, I deliberately take a few moments before I start writing to remind myself of that.

What about: 'I can only write when I have a scary deadline and I'm down to the wire?' I've been there in other jobs, but I don't want to live it every day for even a month. That way lies anxiety and bad writing. Take it a day at a time: the writing will accumulate.

How many words per day?

For *The Rosie Result* I set my daily target at a thousand words (fifteen hundred at a stretch) but I didn't stop when I was on a roll. Occasionally, I'll write four thousand words. There are some who can churn out more, and do it day after day. But I think the more moderate pace allows for more reflection and less stress. And if you rush the work, you'll pay for it in more rewriting.

At the other extreme, I think 250 to 300 words per day is a sensible minimum target. Most writers can do that in an hour (not counting the time set aside for creative thinking), and if you can't devote an hour to your writing at this critical stage, you may have trouble maintaining continuity. At that pace you'll have a draft in under a year, which may sound like forever, but talk to published authors about how long it takes! And you'll have the first chapter in around two weeks, and the second in another two weeks...

You'll soon have an idea of how many words you write per beat, and be able to estimate your total word count for the book. If your rate has you coming in a bit under or over the eighty-thousand-word norm, it's no big deal. Redrafting may add or subtract words, and the length is only a guide. Don't add padding for fear of not reaching a word target.

But if you find that you're *way* out (and don't worry about that yet: it doesn't happen often), the problem is going to be either in the outline or in your writing—or the way one serves the other.

My rule of thumb of 700 words per beat seems to be pretty typical of contemporary writing, but doesn't allow for extremes: *Kim spends fifty minutes telling her life story to the therapist* (technically a single scene but if you're going to include all the dialogue it's going to be a long one). *Don hits a bollard while parking Phil's car* (that beat could be just a few words, its brevity highlighting Don's casualness about what he's done).

If there's a mix of short and long—and variation is good—they'll average out. But if you've got a consistent problem, start with getting some feedback on your prose. Is it too terse or too wordy? Some writers do write more description and reflection, while others strive for pace. If you're happy that your prose is where you want it to be, one option is to accept that your book will be unusually short or long. Such books certainly exist and some have been hugely successful critically and / or commercially. But if you're a debut author, a long novel in particular can be difficult to sell.

The second option is to revise the outline to produce a novel of a more standard length. That may mean going back to the cards, culling or generating more. It will be work, but less work than finding you're at two hundred thousand words and still in the first act. And you'll know for next time.

Overview of the process
A word on getting started: that first sentence and first paragraph.

As I was completing the outline for *The Rosie Result*, I had a trip to Dublin, where I was fortunate enough to be invited to drinks at the house in which James Joyce set his acclaimed story *The Dead*.

I thought it would be a wonderful place to formally begin the new novel, so I took my computer along. I'd been thinking about the opening for some time and had settled on just two words: *Multiple problems*. Pithy and very much Don's voice, I felt. I ceremonially typed them at the dining table and put my computer away.

I'd reckoned without redrafting. In the published book, in line with my earlier comments about creating a memorable opening image, the first sentence reads: *I was standing on one leg shucking oysters when the problems began.* It was probably about the tenth version, and a reminder that our first draft is no more than that—a first draft. Openings almost always change. Get one down and move on. And accept that it can be a bit creaky at first.

Here's my diary entry from the first day of drafting:

> *1100 words but a feeling they're overwritten. A real struggle getting started. Added the oyster-knife incident to set up 'pride comes before a fall' but this will need to pay off down the track to earn its place so early in the book. Only minimally funny. Remainder of chapter should list the five big problems (200 words each?) and then give us the inciting incident—phone call from snow. Hopefully once we hit the Alleged Racist Incident we can start telling the story a bit more fluidly. Looking at that for Day 3 while I get the car serviced.*

And here's Day 3's entry (while I was apparently getting the car serviced):

Wrote chapter 2 (most of the day on this, but 2456 words). Total
5600 words. Did not include the (important) bit in the lecture
scene about Charlie suggesting Don plead Asperger's—feel we
need some time with Hudson to avoid this set-up story taking over.

If you were worried that the outline would be a straitjacket, you can
see that even this early in the writing, I'm making changes to it. No
matter how much time you've spent on your outline, your plot and
characters will evolve as you write.

Spending a full day with just one or two beats is going to show
up stuff that you missed when you were reviewing cards. Just filling
in the detail will create story—including neat things that can add
to the set-ups and pay-offs. Remember to update the outline if you
have ideas for parts of the story yet to be written.

I find that the further I progress, the more I deviate from the
outline. The first quarter tends to follow pretty closely; the middle
half has more invention; and by the time I get to the third act, I'm
incorporating new ideas that have emerged during the writing.

There is an interplay between where I've decided to take my
characters and where they end up taking me, but the major characters'
arcs don't generally change significantly. Writers are often asked:
'Do you know the ending when you start?' I know *an* ending—an
outline isn't complete without one—but it can change, either because
of a late (but not uncommon) decision to redesignate it as a 'false
ending', as discussed in Organising the Story (Chapter 9), or because,
after all the set-up and complications, I think there's a better final
decision or outcome.

I've usually set up alternative endings (driven by decisions!) so
the reader won't be able to see what's coming. That balance and
uncertainty is available for me to exploit as I hit the final pages. So,

as usual, you're not bound by the outline if you can find a better way—and with endings that does happen.

In *The Best of Adam Sharp*, our protagonist could have chosen to stay with his partner, to run off with his old lover or to walk away from both, and my tweaking to accommodate any of those would have been limited to the last two or three chapters.

As I write a scene, I become conscious of whether it could be set up better. Often that means a quick detour to an earlier passage to insert a line or two that will make the current events more plausible: 'I should have seen that coming, but didn't,' says the reader.

When I was describing how to write the outline, I didn't suggest that you include chapter breaks. Some writers do, and you may be asked for an outline broken into chapters if you're applying for a writers' workshop or other support. I'm not going to stop you, though I suggest you feel free to add in extra breaks or skip some as you write.

I find it easier to insert them on the fly, at points that feel natural. My chapters tend to run between one thousand and four thousand words, and if I'm under eight hundred words, I'm inclined to insert a section break and keep going. But don't stress about it: there are few things easier to fix.

Planning your writing day

I'm going to describe my usual writing day. You might like to use it as a starting point for planning your own.

1. Coffee, stretches and a *quick* review of overnight emails. It's hard to write with a clear head if you think there might be life-changing news sitting in your inbox.

2. Review of the previous day's writing. By doing this, I'm
    putting myself back in the story, getting oriented for the day,
    making some progress. Getting past the fear of the blank page.
    I'm also giving my first draft a second look, and I'll find plenty
    to tidy. Sometimes I can be at it for an hour or so if I see a
    better way of doing something.

3. Look at the next few beats in the outline—enough story to
    easily hit my daily word goal. Sometimes, it's just one beat,
    seldom more than three.

4. Creative time. I walk or jog forty minutes, a familiar route
    along quiet roads and parkland near home. I think about
    those beats, and about the criteria for a good scene (listed in
    Chapter 10), especially the idea that each scene should be a
    little story in its own right. And about conflict and reversals
    and references to other scenes.

    I say, aloud: *Trust the process*. If you've been making time
    for creativity, you'll trust the process too, even if for the first
    twenty minutes you don't come up with anything. I don't
    believe I've ever finished the walk without having at least one
    new idea about the scenes I'm going to write. Creativity being
    what it is, I may have ideas on other matters: if they relate to
    the previous day's work, as they often do, I deal with them
    immediately on returning. If they apply to another part of
    the manuscript I've already written, I make the change if it's
    simple (or if it's complex and I can't summarise it in a note) or
    write an in-text note for when I redraft. Anything else for the
    current book goes into the outline.

5. I shower, have breakfast and get down to writing the day's
    beats. Before I type the first words, I remind myself that the

day's job isn't huge. I know what I'm going to write. I've done this before, many times. No pressure. I'm going to enjoy it.

6. I write as well as I can but keep going even if it isn't great. I silence my inner critic. *You can come back to it. Just get the story down.*

7. If the going gets tough, I don't walk away. I don't want to feel I have that option. I lower my standards and get it down—'it' being enough to progress the story as per the outline. Exposition, clunky dialogue, whatever it takes. *Don't get it right, get it done.* Just tell the story. If it lacks drama, or comedy or emotion or whatever you're looking for, you can fix it later. It's almost always easier to improve something that's already in place.

    There have been times when I've felt I was writing so badly that I'd have to throw all the material away, and the next day been surprised that the writing was not as bad as it felt at the time. (Conversely, work of seeming genius doesn't always look so great in the light of morning.)

    Occasionally, I can't seem to get a scene down at all. I usually find that it's trying to do too much—take two or more aspects of the story forward, or provide a home for one of my 'darlings' that doesn't have to be in that particular scene. I kill the darlings (and look for another home for them), then break what's necessary into multiple beats in the outline—which I may then relocate.

8. If I get totally stuck—realise that the beat I'm writing shouldn't even be in the story or just can't find any way of writing it—my last resort is to find a later beat, an easy one, and write that. I'm still moving the manuscript along on

schedule, and I can use tomorrow's creative time (plus the time I'm going to spend lying awake) to start thinking about the issue that stopped me. It doesn't happen often.

9. Even as a seasoned author, I celebrate the end of each act, sometimes with a drink, sometimes with a mental pat on the back.

10. The rest of life. I try hard to schedule everything non-writing, and that creative-time drink, for after I've done my writing work. It's an acknowledgment that writing is my primary job. When I had a day job, it was tougher—but if ever I was going to take time off to write, drafting was the stage to do it in. Then I couldn't afford to waste that hard-earned opportunity.

I do this every single day, without fail, never giving myself an excuse not to write. I'm kidding. We're all human. And anyway, I'd suggest taking a couple of days between acts to reflect on the one just written and to read the full outline of the one you're about to start.

There's also the problem of life intruding, or of discovering that your outline isn't giving you adequate guidance or has problems. Issues and gaps that you didn't see when you were reviewing the cards become apparent when you're devoting a full day to a single one of them. Here's my diary from just into Act 2b of *The Rosie Result*.

Day 34: Ran out of steam. 500 words.

Day 35: Zilch. Need to reread the outline. Feeling it's gone flat, but did some walking & thinking and attended genetics / ethics seminar: can Don be bored with his work—can Blanche ask if there's a cure for albinism…Don wants to be out there in gene editing but has to reinvent himself. Major thoughts on

> *the bar—a geek bar? 'The Science Library': Amghad says,*
> *'What sort of bar would you like to go to?'*
>
> *Day 36: 500 words, mainly in 2a setting up changes to bar stuff.*
>
> *Day 37: Back in 2a, writing the bar-design scene. 46k words.*
> *Added 1k to 2a.*
>
> *Day 38: Back in 2b, writing what feels like filler. Reviewed the*
> *outline—not much inspiration there. Definite feeling of too*
> *many strands. Lots of dull bits and pieces but 4k words done.*

As you can see, I was struggling, losing confidence in what was ahead, and my creative-thinking time was not yet delivering any answers. Instead, I was getting ideas for the previous act—the incubation period doing its thing. I kept moving by going back and making those Act 2a changes. As it turned out, the idea of an autism-friendly bar was a big contribution to the story, so even though I felt I was stuck at the time, I was making important progress.

The next few diary entries are similarly grim—just pushing to write something, without much confidence in it, while my routine was interrupted by stressing over MCing a wedding and speaking at a writers' festival.

Then, after the festival:

> *Day 48: On the plane home. Alex Miller said in the taxi: first draft*
> *is shit, you've got to put it aside and wait for it to call you.*
> *Rereading, it's not so bad. Filled in some more useful stuff re*
> *Blanche and Nadia without hitting the 2nd Act turning-point*
> *material. 1500 words—now 14.5k into 2b in 16 days. Pulling*
> *it back!*

And here I am now, playing the role that my fellow author played for me in the taxi: reassuring you that there will be tough times with your manuscript, but that it's normal and you'll come through.

The first draft of *The Rosie Result* took me sixty-six days. My biggest day was 4700 words, at the start of Act 3. Those sixty-six days included five days of between-act reviews, three days supporting friends and family, and four when my father died. And two days when I just got stuck. Act 1 went the quickest, Act 2b the slowest. That's pretty typical. My four quarters were close to equal length, though it seemed that Act 2b might need some new material (or Acts 1, 2a and 3 might need tightening).

Act 1:	22,000
Act 2a:	21,000
Act 2b:	18,000
Act 3:	21,200
Total:	*82,200*

I was happy. If you're happy with the *shape* of what you've written, you should be too. Rewriting will sort out the details.

On one occasion, I got to this point and wasn't happy (the book was *The Rosie Effect*). I put the evolved outline back on cards and went back to Organising the Story (Chapter 9). If you find yourself in the same situation, don't despair: you're likely to keep most of your writing, but it may need some cutting and pasting. When you redo Reviewing the Outline (Chapter 10), you can skip the beats that you're happy with.

That's the process from a procedural point of view. The next chapter looks at the same stage from the perspective of craft.

12
First Draft—Content

I **deliberated over** whether to include this chapter at all. I could have called it 'What They *Do* Teach You at Writing School', because text on the page is typically what is taught, workshopped and assessed. And, to be fair, this is the skill that needs the most practice, so, even if courses underplay some aspects of novel writing, time devoted to improving prose is time well spent.

The previous chapter outlined a process for producing a first draft. You can now take that process, modify it to suit your circumstances and get on with writing as well as you can, unencumbered by worrying about plot and character development. Your planning will have delivered a story that's structured the way you want it and characters who interact with the story through credible, well-motivated decisions.

But I've found that there are a few areas that regularly bother students, including some experienced writers. So, in the spirit of Elmore Leonard, Kurt Vonnegut and many other writers—but with a bit more elaboration—here are my ten tips on drafting.

1. *First person has its merits.* Third-person close, past tense is
    the most common choice, and I don't think I've ever heard a
    reader say they had a problem with it. However, some readers
    have an aversion to first person, so you need to have a reason
    for going with it. There are some excellent reasons. I've
    written all my novels (though not all my short stories) in first
    person, and here I am on the page again, using 'I' rather than
    a detached textbook style.

    I chose first person for Don Tillman for three reasons.
    First, I wanted the reader to see the world through his eyes:
    the books are about his atypical perspective and I wanted that
    to be on the page as much as possible.

    Second—and closely related—I wanted the story to be
    told in his voice, which again is a little offbeat; but the more of
    it I had, the more subtle I could be about it. If I'd only used it
    in dialogue, I'd have needed to amp it up to compensate.

    Finally, I could create an *unreliable narrator*, not someone
    who's deliberately lying to us or withholding information
    (though that is an option), but a person whose world view is
    different from most readers' and narrators'—and at times, by
    their standards, naive. He can miss things that the reader will
    pick up from reading between the lines. A common choice
    of unreliable narrator is a child who knows less about the
    world—and the implications of what they are reporting—
    than the reader.

    It's often said that dramatic irony, where the reader
    knows something that the narrator doesn't know, is not
    possible in first person, but an unreliable narrator can do the
    job. Similarly, they can create suspense by communicating,
    unknowingly, that there is some threat.

In first person, unless you're writing memoir, your own voice will never be on the page. Some authors feel that this will deny them the opportunity to make full use of their descriptive skills. But the authentic rendition of a character's voice has its own charms. Literary prize winners with distinctive first-person voices include *Life of Pi*, *True History of the Kelly Gang* and *The Testaments* (which is told from three points of view). Margaret Atwood originally wrote *Alias Grace* in third person, but it didn't work for her, so she changed it to first. If you're still in doubt, third-person close.

2. *Present tense can work as your primary tense*. Present tense feels cinematic, modern and immediate, and sometimes literary. In a few years, it may also feel dated! I've seen it argued that if present tense is your base, it can be difficult to break out (temporarily) into other tenses. I haven't found that a problem.

   The Best of Adam Sharp (base tense: simple past) begins, 'If my life before 15 February, 2012 had been a song…' (past conditional) and ends 'Charlie would stay on until the Tuesday…' (future in the past).[8] Fancy tenses, but if my base had been present tense, I'd probably have opened with 'If my life before 15 February, 2012 was a song…' and finish with 'Charlie will stay on…' Entirely workable.

   If you're in doubt about voice and tense, try writing a chapter in each of your different options. It's much more about the feeling of the prose than about anything that can be explained simply or translated into rules, and you'll quickly get a sense of how your options play out on the page.

---

[8] I'm not consciously thinking much about tense when I'm drafting, and certainly not in such technical terms.

3. *Forget the reader—it's you.* Thinking about the reader at this point is only going to be distracting. You made whatever decisions you needed to about likely audience when you settled on concept, structure and style. Now get on with writing.

   If there's a reader I'm thinking about, it's me. Authors may tell you that they laugh at their own jokes and cry at the emotional moments. Fair enough: if we can't please ourselves, we're unlikely to please others.

   There's an exception. Don't assume the reader will have the same response to jokes, politics and (particularly) music as you do. By all means mention them, even showcase them, but don't expect their mere mention to communicate anything beyond that. Do it too much and it can seem lazy—delegating the writing work to Bob Dylan and Tom Waits. Avoiding song lyrics will also save you from messy copyright issues. (If you do decide to use them, flag them so your publisher knows. Copyright on lyrics is very strict—don't assume anything.)

   You can make occasional 'inside baseball' references that will be apparent only to the specialist reader (if they notice them at all), as long as they're bonuses and not essential to plot or character. But they're usually self-indulgent. Unless your book becomes a classic—or cult classic—you can expect them to be overlooked by most of your readers, and possibly lost in foreign-language translations. (Did anyone notice the Madame Bovary references in *The Best of Adam Sharp*? Or why I chose *Running on Empty* as the album Don listened to on repeat on his road trip?)

4. *Keep a low profile*. In fact, aim for invisibility. It's related to Elmore Leonard's cardinal rule: *If it sounds like writing, I rewrite it.* I don't want my readers to be conscious of me—and how well or badly I write—while they're reading. I want them to be immersed in the story and the characters and the prose without admiring how I did it or thinking of me for any reason. When I'm co-writing with my partner, Anne, I don't want the reader to be conscious of whose words they're reading. When they're finished, they're welcome to reflect on what a good job I or we did, but only then.

   Yes, there are writers who are there on the page, dazzling us with their cleverness: the simile that's so original that we stop to admire it; breaking the fourth wall, as Kurt Vonnegut does in *Breakfast of Champions*, announcing that he, the author, is the only person who can change the hero's fate. We see it particularly in comedy, and if you're as good at it as Kathy Lette and Douglas Adams, you'll doubtless win a following, but will probably still alienate some readers. If you're not good at it, you'll look like you're straining for effect. As a writer of comedy, I'd advise you to let the characters create the fun, and to give them the brilliant observations and one-liners.

5. *Jump into the story.* Don't be afraid of starting a scene or chapter *in medias res*—in the middle of things. The term is more often applied to a story as a whole, but it's a valuable technique throughout. It's almost automatic to start a chapter by setting time and place, and perhaps recapping events. But your readers have grown up on a diet of movies and television where story is often cut to its essence. They are accustomed to filling in the gaps.

In *The Rosie Result*, Chapter 2 begins with a formulaic introduction to time and place: *By the following June…* But Chapter 3's opening (*The phone call…came at 10.18*) takes us directly into new action and Chapter 4 (*The GPS indicated a drive of three hours and eighteen minutes*) picks up the expected next scene without recapping. Chapter 5 takes it up a level, going straight in with untagged dialogue: '*What the fuck is that supposed to mean?*' The next sentence explains—*I was back in Melbourne, debriefing Rosie*—and we realise from context and voice that the dialogue is Rosie's, but it's a punchier start than if I'd written the two sentences in the more natural order.

A line of dialogue is one of the easiest ways of doing this, and the reader will get what you're doing. Mix it up. At the scene level, there's no need for preliminaries that our reader can work out, unless they're genuinely pertinent to character or plot. If Don and Rosie have been summoned to see Hudson's principal, we can leave out the journey to the school and the walk down the corridor and maybe even the summons that brought them there. That is, unless we need to set up how far away the school is, or if Don is going to have a flashback to his own schooldays as he walks the corridor, or if Don and Rosie are going to argue about which of them goes to the meeting.

6. *Learn to handle dialogue.* One of the things that held me back from writing novels was a lack of confidence that I could write dialogue: not the content, but the formatting. In the end it wasn't hard to learn the rules and my concerns seem ridiculous in hindsight. But I've found many aspiring authors have the same problem and avoid direct dialogue.

So, we get this: *When Sonia asked if he was all right, Hudson said that he wasn't and didn't want to return to Australia or to change schools.*

Which, in direct dialogue, can be:

'Are you all right, Hudson?' said Sonia.

'No. I don't want to go to Australia. I don't want to change schools. I don't want to change anything.'

Far more immediate and engaging. We hear the characters' voices and get to know them a little better as a result. I'm not saying that you should never use indirect dialogue—variety is the spice—but formatting direct dialogue is not hard. Read some samples from novels you'd like to emulate, noting punctuation and (if they're modern) observance of the widely agreed conventions:

a. Use 'he said / she said / Don said' after (or occasionally before) speech, and only as often as necessary to clearly identify the speaker. If there are just two people in the conversation, the alternation, voices and what is being said can make it obvious who's speaking, and you'll need few of these dialogue / speech tags. Crime writer Stuart McBride, for example, doesn't use them at all, and that's something to aspire to.

b. Use adverbs ('he said, angrily') sparingly, and substitutions for 'said' and 'asked' ('interjected', 'exclaimed', 'hissed') even more sparingly, if at all. Mix it up with action tags: *Hudson nodded. 'Same thing happened at school.'* Be watchful of overusing drinking and smoking actions for your action tags (more of a temptation if you're a drinker or smoker).

c.   Dialogue needs to be not only natural, but true to the
     speaker. It's important that characters don't all sound
     like you. I don't picture characters in my mind, but I do
     try to imagine them speaking, often drawing on people
     I know. Informal expressions can indicate a character's
     origins and age. Just a few can help in characterising and
     differentiating; conversely, getting them wrong will jar
     with readers. 'Bloody hell' will sound authentic from a
     seventy-year-old English or Australian character, but not
     an American millennial.

d.   Handle accents or dialect with a light touch. You can set
     the scene early with a couple of pronunciations to trigger
     the reader's recognition, but after that there's a risk
     you'll annoy them, especially if you lean on well-worn
     stereotypes. They *get* that Liam O'Shea is Irish and that
     international student Wang Yu may speak English with
     an accent. But you can show this through choice of words
     and expressions appropriate to their culture, education
     and profession, again sparingly. I'm Australian but I don't
     call anyone 'cobber'.

     As always, there are successful exceptions, like
     Trainspotting, with its consistent misspellings to render
     dialect.[9] Just know that if you go down that route, you are
     likely to lose some readers.

7. *Don't have your characters state the obvious*. Sometimes you
    have to convey information that wouldn't arise naturally in
    conversation. If the information is known to all parties, it's

---

[9]   So-called eye dialect, because the reader sees it rather than hears it.

unlikely it would be stated, except in a situation of conflict (which is a good way to do it: *You slept with her. I can't believe it: you slept with her. In the home where our* children *live. When you were supposed to be visiting your mother. Your mother, who has* cancer...) Alternatively, we can show it through action or the protagonist can tell us directly.

A similar rule applies to communicating thoughts and feelings. Your protagonist can tell the reader what's going on in their head, directly, but, assuming you're writing in first person or third-person close, none of your other characters can unless they vocalise it. You need to ask whether they would actually do so in real life: people far more often show or imply their emotions than state them in unsubtle ('on-the-nose') dialogue: *Since we split up, I've been feeling angry but it's because I miss you and all the things we used to do.* It's better—and usually more faithful to real life—to communicate the emotions in subtext, through action or elliptical speech. *'I'm doing fine—not wasting my time playing Scrabble,' he said, and slammed the door behind him.*

8. *Locate your story.* Your characters have to move around in their world: their home, their place of work, the towns and countryside where the story is set. Make sure the readers know where they are and what they're doing. Don't leave them as talking heads in a void.

    It adds to your cognitive load and distracts from your writing to conjure up and remember (for example) an imaginary house. If you make it up on the fly, you run the risk that you'll have a character walking down the hallway to their bedroom at one point and then upstairs to it at another.

At least I do. So, I try to set my stories in familiar places, and when there's an interior that features in the story, I base it on a real one.

In *The Best of Adam Sharp*, almost all of the second half of the story takes place in a French holiday house: I used a real house that I reoriented so Adam could watch the sunset from the balcony. The British author Emma Healey let me use her residence as the model for Adam's home in England. If you're only visiting once, make a sketch plan. One author I know collects floor plans and photos from real-estate inspections.

9. *Use the environment.* The physical environment, natural and built, is not just an opportunity for you to display your powers of description but another means of supporting the story by conveying (or counterpointing) atmosphere, mood and the passing of time. If you're describing it from a character's point of view, you have the interplay between who they are (and their emotional state) and what they observe.

   In *Two Steps Forward* and *Two Steps Onward*, Anne and I worked to synchronise the moods of these stories of long-distance walks with the environment and seasons: traversing barren terrain; walking in the rain; coming into spring. We were also able to contrast the perceptions of our protagonists, an artist and an engineer, in their first-person descriptions.

10. *Be specific.* Try to avoid general statements, particularly of behaviour. Show us some with enough context for us to deduce that it happens all the time. I've already emphasised the value of preferring scenes to summaries when working toward an outline, but it applies at the sentence level, too.

Not only does the example make the writing more vivid, by providing the reader with something they can picture, but it makes you work harder on understanding the story and characters. *Hudson was having problems at school.* What problems? Show us one, or two or three. Creating them will give us more material to work with. If Hudson gets lost finding his way to the school gate, we know something specific and unexpected about his disabilities, and we have an incident to refer to later.

These are just tips—a few to add to and compare with the many already out there. There's no shortage of advice on how to write prose, and an almost unlimited number of models in the form of great books.

So, write as well as you've learned to do, and, if you're like most authors, you'll have periods of disillusionment, but also a deserved sense of satisfaction when you hold a completed draft in your hand. You've written a novel or memoir. Chances are, you'll feel good not only about finishing, but about the quality of what you've written. Take a little time to savour the moment.

Because the bad news is that it still has a long way to go. That's also the good news: by the time you finish revising, your manuscript will be better than you could imagine now.

The next chapter is about making that improvement.

13
Rewriting

At the end of this stage, you'll have:

1. A revised manuscript (ready for submission, if appropriate).

At my first big public reading, on World Book Night in London, I found myself sitting on a sofa in the green room with a novelist whose book was topping the bestseller lists. I was silently rehearsing the passage I'd chosen from *The Rosie Project* (one that I hoped showcased my best writing) and, red pen in hand, was noting small improvements—edits that could still be made after more than seventy passes, and the input of my Australian, British, American, Canadian and German editors. I sneaked a look at my fellow author and saw that she was doing the same thing. *You can always make it better.*

At this stage of my career, I could probably devote less effort to this stage, in the expectation that my manuscript would be accepted anyway, and rely on my editors to pick up what I'd missed. But I want to give them the best starting point I can, so that their time and expertise is not wasted on identifying problems that I could find for myself.

Writing authorities, whether pantsers or planners, largely agree on the maxim that good writing is rewriting. And at this point, we've rejoined the pantsers. The redrafting process is much the same for everyone, though we'd hope to have less work to do on structure, having done a lot already.

Having shut down your inner critic, the time has come to give it full reign. You'll be pleasantly surprised by the quality of some of your writing: pat yourself on the back and reassure yourself of your capabilities. And you'll be shocked at how bad some of it is: remind yourself that, starting from such a low base, it will be easy to improve.

After the rush of getting the draft done, you need to take a second and third and…how many looks? These days I'd expect to go right through the draft at least seven, perhaps as many as twelve times, before submitting to my publisher. If it's your first novel, expect to do more.

This is—or should be—satisfying work: you're making it better. It's often only now that you find what the story is really about—the big themes and character arcs that you've incorporated subconsciously. That discovery will likely prompt changes to strengthen those new-found aspects of the story.

You don't need to allocate big chunks of time to your rewriting. Just mark where you're up to and restart from there when you're ready. And if you have spare time, do a bit more. As ideas occur, you're free to drop into the text at any point and incorporate them.

Reviewing the big picture

Before you start a read-through of your manuscript, reread Chapter 9 of this book, about reviewing your outline. Your story has now been fleshed out and the shape has likely evolved too. Act lengths no longer need to be estimated by counting cards but can be measured in words. In other respects, the same advice applies. It provides a good basis for an initial big-picture review of your manuscript. You may find yourself deciding to make cuts, generate more story or reorganise. Resist the temptation to pad out a too-short act by adding superfluous words.

If you feel the story's not working—it happens—or the structure can be improved, go back to the outline or, better, lay it all out on cards again. You can reuse the ones you wrote originally, but I'd recommend redoing them from the manuscript or outline. Play with them in the knowledge that shifting blocks of text around is not hard and fixing up the continuity can be surprisingly straightforward. You can do this for individual chapters, too. Console yourself by imagining what a pantser would be doing at this point. And, as always, remind yourself that you're making your manuscript better.

Where to focus

In my first pass, my primary concern is to establish whether the story is working, or whether I may need to make major changes—possibly going back to the outline or cards.

I want to see how the story hangs together: are there plot holes, big moments not set up, passages that don't add anything? I'm also looking for opportunities to reuse details to give a stronger sense of cohesion—of each passage contributing to the whole. Rosie was at the hairdresser when she was unexpectedly summoned to work, so later that evening when she arrives at Hudson's graduation, Don can observe in his distinctive way that her hair seems to be in two different shades.

I take the opportunity to (temporarily) name my chapters. Names are easier to remember than numbers, which are also likely to change as I review chapter breaks. They make me think about what each chapter is contributing to the whole. *The Genetics Lecture Outrage*; *Opening Night at the Bar*; *Hudson's Graduation*.

In this first pass, you'll find all the kinds of small stuff I've listed below; though there will be more passes, you might as well fix the problems as you find them. Take pleasure in doing so: even if you're just correcting a misplaced apostrophe, you're making the manuscript unequivocally better. And pick up any changes you've made to the outline but not to the text.

I suggest you then put the manuscript aside for about two weeks—longer is even better if you're not under deadline pressure. This is a good time to work on something else, to help another writer, to re-emerge into the world after the intensity of drafting. You'll return with fresh eyes and be amazed when you look at your manuscript again—amazed in both good and bad ways.

I try to have a theme or two for each subsequent read—something to keep front of mind, though I'm still looking for all the other issues.

I'll always do a pass to check for reader engagement: why should they keep reading? What dramatic questions are in play right now? What is the reader sticking around to learn? This combines well with a review of key decisions—which, as we know, are frequently tied to turning points. We want them to be as surprising, powerful and revealing of character as we can make them. Generally, a decision will have more impact if taken deliberately, in one moment, rather than in smaller steps, though such steps can lead up to it. Can we make it more difficult? The more our decision-maker must sacrifice, the more courage they need, the stronger the decision. Can we show, rather than tell? Can we move it from dialogue to a physical action that makes the reader work a little harder?

When I was writing the screenplay for *The Rosie Project*, I was focused on Don Tillman's—my protagonist's—arc. Then someone said to me, 'Imagine Jennifer Lawrence reading this script with a view to playing Rosie. She won't be thinking much about Don: only whether everything Rosie says and does is authentic and motivated.'[10]

I got into the habit of rereading my scripts from the perspective of at least the second-most-important character, and occasionally another. It's a practice I've brought to my novels, recognising that some readers will identify with a secondary character and, more importantly, that everyone in a story should behave in a credible way.

In *The Rosie Result*, I read for Hudson and Rosie. Editing *The Best of Adam Sharp*, a love quadrangle, I read for all four.

Another worthwhile theme is finessing minor characters who've been introduced during the writing process for some narrative purpose: to serve a drink, to provide a character with a family or friend, to interrupt the prospective lovers before they can get together. Our immediate thought as we draft is likely to be a stereotype. Now we can look at making the characters consolidate their place in the novel by being original and interesting. If they've grown with the story rather than being defined in advance, check for consistency and opportunities to set up traits that are important later.

Try doing a pass with a printed document (even if you make the edits directly to the electronic manuscript as you go). If that helps you see things you hadn't noticed before, you may want to use a printed version in further passes (try changing the font if you're printing more than once, to keep your eyes fresh).

---

[10] Jennifer Lawrence eventually did read the script for *The Rosie Project*, and apparently liked it enough to accept the role of Rosie in the movie. As with so many things in the movie-production world, the deal fell through.

For the final pass, I suggest reading aloud, preferably to someone like your long-suffering partner or a writer who owes you a favour. It'll take a few sessions, but you'll find small stuff that you skipped over before, and possibly some passages that bore you and your listener to tears. Another option is to use a digital read-aloud function (Microsoft Word has one). The software won't make the unconscious corrections that your human reader sometimes will: you'll hear every typo and repeated word.

What to look for

Here are some things I look for in every pass (and every time I edit any part of a manuscript), besides the obvious targets of spelling, grammar and any way you can see of telling your story better. Your mindset should be that every time you close the document, you've improved it, even if only in a small way.

1. Almost everybody overwrites in the first draft. Using fewer words to say the same thing makes the writing more concentrated and powerful. Individual cuts may seem minor, but the accumulation can be substantial in both word count and effect. It's worth approaching the manuscript with the intention of reducing words (the experience of trimming a short story, essay or opinion piece to meet a word limit will pay off here).

    Rather than asking yourself 'Is this good?', ask 'Is it necessary?' In the first thousand words or so, ask this question firmly, and if the answer is yes, follow up with 'Could it come later?' You don't need to force-feed the reader background information at this point: just the minimum they need to understand what's going on. Save the witty observations and reflections on life for when the story is rolling along.

Don't worry about making your manuscript too short: you'll be adding new material as ideas arise, and the net effect is likely to be an increase in length. After two passes of *The Rosie Result*, where I found lots of opportunities to trim, new material had pushed it from 83,000 to 87,400 words.

There is always some low-hanging fruit:

a. Trim your scenes (and indeed all beats). It's a screen-writing maxim that you can usually lose the first and last lines of a scene with no impact except making it punchier. We've already talked about coming in late (*in medias res*). At the other end, it's a common fault to add just one more sentence to the passage after it has already reached a strong conclusion.

b. Get to know your personal overwriting habits. I slip in 'of course' and 'in fact' too often, and frequently begin dialogue with 'So' or 'Well'. A global search will give me a bunch of opportunities for deletions. Check for words or phrases you overuse and change accordingly. While you're at it, find all the exclamation marks. Almost always, they're better deleted.

c. Stay alert for wordy phrases that can be compressed: *painting a picture of* becomes *portraying*; *requires some level of discipline* becomes *requires discipline*. 'Management speak' has no place in a novel, unless managers are speaking.

d. Say it once. Worse than telling instead of showing is doing both. This happens particularly when the information is obvious from the dialogue but is then repeated in a speech tag (or adverb), or as simple exposition. *Her good mood vanished instantly. 'Screw you!' she yelled angrily*. In dialogue, be brutal: if you can do without the commentary, do without it. Let the dialogue flow, as it does in the real world. A comment following a dramatic action or statement will often reduce its power. After *Screw you*, we don't need *Ouch* or *Now I was in trouble*.

e. Kill those adjectives and (especially) adverbs. *Very* and *just* can often go, as can modifiers habitually attached to certain verbs and nouns without adding anything— *eminently* suitable, *blatantly* obvious, *absolutely* certain. Other times you can look for a single noun or verb that does the job: *walked slowly* can become *ambled* or *strolled*.

f. When we're communicating the thoughts of the protagonist, it's generally unnecessary to say *I* (or *he / she*) *saw*, *heard*, *thought* and so on. *I saw that Hudson had purchased new shoes* can likely be compressed to *Hudson had purchased new shoes*.

2. First thoughts are clichés. That's fine for a first draft: you captured the sense of what you wanted to say. Now, keep the sense but get rid of 'force to be reckoned with' and 'like a ton of bricks' (at least in narration: you may want to keep such expressions in dialogue for characterisation). The same applies to minor characters: as noted earlier, first thoughts are often stereotypes. Fix those things you threw down with the intention of coming back to later but then forgot about: names of people and fictional organisations (check they're not real), words you were too busy to look up.

3. If you find yourself struggling over a passage, not being able to find the right words, ask: 'Do I need this at all?' Surprisingly often, the solution is *select, delete*. If it isn't, you'll have gained a better understanding of why you need the passage—what it's doing to advance the story—which will likely help you to find a way to fix it.

4. Make sure any foreshadowing (*I was standing on one leg shucking oysters when the problems began* and *I may have found a solution to the wife problem*) is necessary. Usually we do it to get the reader interested in reading on, with a sense of anticipation, curiosity, even dread. In these examples, I was also looking for a strong opening. But it breaks up the flow and can often be dropped.

5. Keep an eye out for active alternatives to passive voice. (If you're not sure about this, time to learn.)

6. Look for word repetition: the same word used two or more times in a short space. It can be done deliberately, for emphasis or poetic effect, but if not, you should find a synonym or rephrase. Even after your multiple passes looking for them, an editor will almost certainly find instances you've missed.

7. Look for two or more sentences in succession structured the same way. *Holding the bike, I assisted Hudson to get on. Pushing it forward, I held onto him.* Again, you can do it deliberately, for effect: it's the accidental, clunky cases we want to eliminate.

8. We've mentioned killing your darlings. This is where it happens. Yes, it's clever, insightful or (this is the one that hurts me most) hilarious, but does it advance story or character? If not…kill. If in doubt, seek a second opinion from someone

you trust—see beta readers below. Chances are, they won't be as attached to that darling as you are.

One thing that can be hard to pick up, particularly when you're going through the manuscript slowly and carefully, is repeated information. I often miss it until I'm nearing my final read, just before submission, and am moving more swiftly, and ask myself 'Didn't I just read something like that an hour ago?'

Other eyes, including your eventual readers, moving more swiftly, are more likely to pick it up. It's one of many good reasons for seeking input from beta readers.

Beta readers

When you've done a pass without finding anything much, or at least feel that the story is firmly set, I'd recommend sending your manuscript to a few beta readers (test readers: the term is from beta testers in information technology).

There are paid manuscript-reading services, but in addition or instead, I'd suggest some reliable friends or writing-group colleagues. More is better, but only if they're going to give you honest feedback and you're prepared to give time to all of it. Human nature and friendship being what they are, such readers are likely to be gentle with you, though it won't always feel that way. Which also means that if they say something is not working, they mean it.

By about your third book, you'll have identified those whose feedback you find most helpful. I peaked at around ten readers, which was an interesting experiment, but a lot of feedback to process! These days it's usually five or six.

Some I choose because I want their feedback on aspects of the book that are not easily researched to the level of credibility that will convince readers who are in the know: voice, settings, vocations, character background. For *The Best of Adam Sharp*, I chose a reader from the North of England to check Adam's Mancunian voice, and a pianist to ensure I'd got the technical and practical aspects of piano-playing right. For *The Rosie Result*, I had two readers with children of Hudson's age—leading to a debate about whether he'd be allowed to travel alone on a Melbourne tram—and a teacher, who helped me with the authenticity of Hudson's teacher, principal and school environment.

Readers assigned these tasks generally love having their expertise recognised and being used in the service of a novel. Don't forget to thank them in the acknowledgments, send them a copy of the book and invite them to the launch.

If you're writing about a minority group that you're not thoroughly familiar with, it's common sense to have a sensitivity reader, though that should be only part of their brief: 'Is this authentic?' is the real question I would be asking. Be clear and correct about payment: the last thing you want to do is add to the exploitation of a community.

If there are aspects of the book's writing that I'm nervous about, I don't usually ask until I've had my readers' unprompted feedback. If they don't mention it, I may then ask, but I don't want my question to encourage readers, especially non-expert ones, to see something that isn't there.

Before you send your draft out, decide on a mechanism for consolidating the feedback. You don't want to have to copy hundreds of annotations on printed manuscripts onto a master file. I ask readers to make comments or tracked changes on a Microsoft Word file, then I use the Compare function to add each marked-up document to the master.

Whether I've engaged a reader for a specialised look or a 'Tell me what you think' open question, I ask them to mark any places where they're bored ('I'd be inclined to skim over this'), riveted ('I couldn't put it down') or confused. The 'riveted' information is less important (you assumed it was all riveting, right?), but gives them a chance to be nice, and hopefully less uncomfortable about pointing out the boring and confusing bits.

If your readers ask, 'Do you want me to flag any typos?' the answer is: 'Yes, please, if it's not too much trouble.' You'll be surprised how many they find, and your manuscript will be in better shape as you begin the final polishing. 'It's still too rough to worry about that' is *not* a good answer. Don't insult your volunteers or waste their time with something that's not already as tidy as you can make it.

I take all feedback seriously, but if two people have identified the same problem, I take it *very* seriously. Two readers out of five or six scales up to a lot of readers of a published book.

These reviews can be a rude awakening, especially if you're not accustomed to submitting your work for criticism. Frequently, they'll identify continuity errors that are not easy to fix. You may be surprised that a reader has misunderstood something you thought was crystal clear (or subtle, but obvious to the thinking person). Plus those 'boring' passages that have to go or be rewritten: not much point publishing material that readers aren't going to read.

Don't take it personally. I'll say it again: *don't take it personally*. You asked for their help, on the basis that you valued their opinion, and they've given it. I've had a good friend whom I'd expected to *love* my manuscript tell me over dinner how disappointed they were in it, and another abandon a novel halfway: 'I could see what was coming.' I didn't feel good about either of them at the time, but I got over it. And when I'd done that, I took their feedback seriously. Don't lose friendships over criticism you've asked for; be grateful that you're learning about the problems now, rather than when your agent or publisher rejects the manuscript because of them.

What I don't feel bound by is advice on how to fix anything. Neil Gaiman neatly summarises what most experienced writers have learned: 'Remember: when people tell you something's wrong or doesn't work for them, they are almost always right. When they tell you exactly what they think is wrong and how to fix it, they are almost always wrong.'

I respect my readers' assessment that there's a problem. But they're readers. I'm the author; I'm the one who's going to decide how I fix it in the context of what I'm trying to do. Suggestions welcome, of course—but I seldom adopt them.

Wrapping up

Most of your rewriting / editing is going to be fairly routine, so you can save your creative time for the bigger problems. You'll find a way through, often using existing elements of the story, sometimes so elegantly that you wonder if the solution was always there in your mind—the way the story was meant to be.

Read it again. Put it aside for a couple of weeks and come back for one more pass. Or two. Because this is it. This is what you're going to send out into the publishing world.

If it's your first book, and you can afford it, pay for a professional edit. (Some publishers will tell you not to bother, but you want everything going for you when they see it.) If you can't afford a full edit, at least get the first chapter (or three chapters, which is what some publishers ask to see initially) done. Check that your freelance editor has experience in your genre and broad style before engaging them, and, if in any doubt, ask them to edit a sample chapter before committing to the full manuscript.

Remember that the person assessing your manuscript for publication is likely to be an editor by profession. If they hit grammar errors, awkward phrasing or unnecessary exposition, they may give up or form a negative view before the story gets moving and your prose settles down.

With beta-reader feedback incorporated, *The Rosie Result* had grown to ninety thousand words. When I hit *send* on my email, eleven months after I'd begun my first attempt at a synopsis, I was reasonably confident it represented close to the best I could do with my concept, my time and my writing abilities. And, thanks to my beta team, I knew that some readers at least would like it. Regardless of what happened now, I'd written, refined and polished a full manuscript.

If you've stayed with me and the process, you've done the same. It's a mighty achievement in itself: for everyone who 'has a book in them' or plans to write a book, or gets to thirty thousand words, only a few get this far. Congratulations. There's a whole business now of getting it published, and I won't offer advice on finding or dealing with publishers and agents, except to say that people in the publishing industry vary in their competence, enthusiasm and (most obviously) taste, but are overwhelmingly decent and honest. Keep that in mind when things aren't going your way.

If your book is acquired by a mainstream publisher, the writing is not over—there's still editing to be done. We'll finish with a few words on that.

But first, give it just one more pass…

14
Working with Your Editor

The great mistake that new—and sometimes experienced—authors make with editing is one of attitude, perhaps a hangover from schooldays or past employment. The editor is not there to grade your work or—once your book been accepted for publication—as a gatekeeper. Their job is to help you make your book better, not as your boss or client, but as your coach. Occasionally they'll get it wrong, or push hard on something you disagree with, but—in general—their interests are the same as yours. They can help make your book significantly better.

My first rule (mentioned in the previous chapter) is not to waste your editor's time with improvements you could have made yourself. That's one reason I use beta readers. When the professional picks up my book, I want all the low-hanging fruit to have been picked, so they have to draw on their best skills to find further improvements.

Then, everything I said in the previous chapter about dealing with feedback from beta readers applies here, including the observation that readers—including professional editors—are much better at spotting problems than coming up with good fixes. You can throw your hands in the air at the solution your editor has suggested, but that's not an excuse to dismiss the problem they identified.

This is particularly true if your editor suggests structural change—or, more accurately, flags a problem that you realise will require structural change to fix. An editing process typically begins with a big-picture structural edit, followed by copy editing—line-level editing—and proofreading. The last two are about detail, and they can sometimes get a bit tedious, but I seldom find much to disagree with or to get rattled about.

Structural edits are more confronting. The good news is that, if you've followed a deliberate structure, the shape of your book is likely to be better than most that your editor sees—possibly good enough that the editor won't have much to say in the structural edit and will move quickly to the next stage. Breathe a sigh of relief.

But when the editor does call for structural change, it's because they've seen issues that don't *appear* to be amenable to a simple, localised fix (remember, you're the solutions person). Perhaps the protagonist is unlikeable, the romantic subplot is not believable or the opening chapters move too slowly.

The Rosie Result's structural edit was verbal: my publisher didn't like the title as submitted (*The Rosie Child*); the start was a bit slow, and the action dragged coming up to the midpoint; Gary the Homeopath was too cardboard-cutout evil (after my best efforts never to portray a character that way); Allannah seemed neglectful of her daughter, Blanche.

My international editors also had some concerns (the larger publishers, after paying substantial advances, expect a seat at the editing table). Not enough of Rosie on the page; Don's continuing use of body mass index in describing women (sexist, fat-shaming); and a serious concern that I was inviting the reader to accept Don's apparent racism in the Genetics Lecture Outrage. That contrasted with feedback from another international editor who had loved that scene and its consequences: 'Great discussion of the issues of difference, including political correctness at the expense of common sense.' I wasn't happy with that response either, as it still implied that I was taking a position.

After a hard look, and some reflection, I acknowledged all of the concerns as legitimate. Fixing them would make the book stronger.

If we have a structure and the language to describe it, we can articulate the problems and perhaps even apply some routine treatments. In relation to the above, I saw 'first act too long', 'lack of escalation in 2a' and 'unmotivated character': not necessarily easy, but familiar—and easier to fix than what I'd already done.

Several of the issues could be dealt with by local changes. My international editors had suggested that all references to body mass index be dropped; instead, I had Don explain that it was a habit that he was trying to overcome and apply it first, in a concerned way, to his male friend Dave. A few local changes explained Gary a little better and normalised Allannah's interactions with her daughter. Some tightening and reorganising of the scenes in Act 2a improved the escalation.

Putting more of Rosie on the page involved generating story. If you have to do that, it may take some creative time, but you'll often be able to leverage existing beats, making the story as a whole more cohesive. It was work for me, but significantly improved the manuscript, as did the other changes.

The Genetics Lecture Outrage problem was more difficult, but again, it wasn't on every page of the book. I reviewed all the scenes in which it was mentioned and added a reconciliation with Don's accuser, with Rosie at its centre—having more of her on the page was on my mind, so my solutions were addressing that at the same time. Then I inserted, right after the actual Genetics Lecture Outrage scene, a conversation between Don and Rosie (again) in which Don is enlightened and chastened.

Quite a bit of writing, but always with the sense of making the manuscript stronger in my own eyes as well as my editors'. I was much happier with the Genetics Lecture Outrage once I was done, moving it from a rather one-sided take that reflected some of my own lazy thinking (my editor was right) to a more nuanced exploration of an important issue.

If the structural edit requires you to rethink sequence, again, don't panic. Cut-and-pastes are mechanically easily, but if the changes involve more than a couple of these, I'd counsel you to go back to the cards, updated as necessary. It doesn't take long, and that visual take on what you've got will make the work easier and may prompt some unrelated improvements.

Once you've got the structural edit sorted, it's likely to be a relatively clear journey to publication. When I get a detailed edit ('copy edit' or 'line edit') back, with comments on almost every paragraph, I take a few minutes to get over 'seeing red'. All those comments can be confronting, but it's a *line edit*—most of it is detail and easily fixed, and (almost) every suggestion will make the book better.

I begin with a pass through to do the easy stuff: grammar, spelling, paragraph breaks, awkward phrasing, word repetition and the like. I skip over the tougher stuff, but I have a good sense of progress, and by the time I'm finished, the remaining mark-up looks much less daunting—especially as I'm doing it electronically, and can delete the suggestions as I deal with them.

Then I get to work on the less-straightforward stuff, right down to doing my creativity routines to deal with any recalcitrant problems, which may be as small as finding the right word or phrase.

Throughout the editing process, I remind myself of the time I spent making 'improvements' to my already-published book before my big public reading: *you can always make it better*.

I wrote my last diary entry for *The Rosie Result* eighteen months after I'd started work on the synopsis and two days before the manuscript went to the printer. It read: *a couple of awkward word reps fixed*. I'd done fourteen complete passes, seven of which were during the editing process. It was published two months later.

A final reminder: this book has been about process, based on what has worked for me. If you've kept a diary and reflected on what parts of it worked for you, what didn't and what you could usefully change—then you're well on your way to defining and refining your own process, tailored to your specific needs, skills and ambitions.

Your next project will be easier.

Acknowledgments

The ideas and techniques presented in this book come from a variety of sources. Many have been around so long that their origins are lost; some are associated with particular writers or pundits, whom I've done my best to acknowledge; some I learned from my teachers, including my fellow writers. A few are my own. My focus has been on selecting what I've found most useful and organising it into a framework.

In Chapter 13, I discussed the value of beta readers, and mentioned I'd peaked at ten. This book confirmed the value and shaded the record: my eleven readers were all writers, from beginners to established novelists. So, very big thanks to Anne Buist (of course and always), Allison Browning, Caris Bizzaca, Tania Chandler, Amy Jasper, Suzanne Kiraly, Kylie Ladd, Lana Nowakowski, Bec Peniston-Bird, Anne Tillig and Fran Willcox.

Even after that input, and ten passes of the manuscript, my editor, David Winter, found plenty of opportunities for improvement. David has been my editor, as well as Anne's and my joint editor, since *The Best of Adam Sharp*. He's the person I'm thinking of when I write about how much a good editor adds to a book, and why they earn the profuse thanks that appear in acknowledgments. Profuse thanks again, David.

The team at Text Publishing, with Michael Heyward at the helm, has stuck with Anne and me through novels, a novella, a recipe book and now this. Their enthusiasm and professionalism have helped us to achieve our vision for the books, and brought them to an international audience.

Finally, as always, Anne has been sounding board, first reader and dedicated partner in the 6.30 p.m. creativity sessions. Without her support, none of these books would have been written.